Asien- und Afrika-Studien
der Humboldt-Universität
zu Berlin

Band 23

2006
Harrassowitz Verlag · Wiesbaden

Peter Acker

Liu Chuxuan (1147–1203)
and his Commentary
on the Daoist Scripture
Huangdi yinfu jing

2006
Harrassowitz Verlag · Wiesbaden

Bibliographische Information der Deutschen Nationalbibliothek
Die Deutsche Nationalbibliothek verzeichnet diese Publikation in der Deutschen
Nationalbibliographie; detaillierte bibliographische Daten sind im Internet
über http://dnb.d-nb.de abrufbar.

Bibliographic information published by the Deutsche Nationalbibliothek
The Deutsche Nationalbibliothek lists this publication in the Deutsche Nationalbibliographie;
detailed bibliographic data are available in the internet
at http://dnb.d-nb.de

For further information about our publishing program consult our
website http://www.harrassowitz-verlag.de

© Otto Harrassowitz GmbH & Co. KG, Wiesbaden 2006
Kreuzberger Ring 7c-d, 65205 Wiesbaden,
produktsicherheit.verlag@harrassowitz.de
This work, including all of its parts, is protected by copyright. Any use
beyond the limits of copyright law without the permission of the
publisher is forbidden and subject to penalty. This applies particularly to
reproductions, translations, microfilms and storage and processing in
electronic systems.

Printed in Germany
ISSN 0948-9789
ISBN 978-3-447-05241-2

Table of Contents

Preface 7

Introduction: Daoism in Contemporary China.. 9
   1. Political perspectives 9
   2. Daoism and Chinese culture 11

1: Inner Alchemy (neidan 內丹) 17
   1. The term *inner alchemy* 17
   2. The theory of reversion 19
   3. Practice: The three treasures and the restoration of primordial *Yang-qi* 24

2: Liu Chuxuan and Early *Quanzhen*-Daoism 29
   1. The emergence of early *Quanzhen*-Daoism 29
   2. Liu Chuxuan's (1147 – 1203) encounter with *Quanzhen* 33
   3. The nature of *Quanzhen*, its basic ideas and teachings 41

3: The *Huangdi Yinfu Jing* and its Significance in *Quanzhen* Daoism 49
   1. Authorship, date and basic content of the scripture 49
   2. The role of the classics and the significance of the *Yinfu jing* in early *Quanzhen* Daoism 54

4: Liu Chuxuan's Commentary and his Theory of Self-Cultivation 59
   1. Introduction 59
   2. The Dao of Heaven and cosmological notions 61
   3. The "three vehicles": A narrative of self-cultivation 67

Conclusion 75

Commentary on *The Yellow Emperor's Scripture of the Hidden Contracts* 77

DZ 122 *Huangdi yinfujing zhu* 111

Bibliography 121
   Abbreviations 121
   1. Primary Sources from the Daoist Canon 121
   2. Other Chinese Sources 122
   3. Secondary Literature in Chinese 122
   4. Secondary Literature in Western Languages 123

Preface

In this study, I will present a complete and annotated translation of a commentary on the Daoist text *Huangdi yinfu jing* 黃帝陰符經(*The Yellow Emperor's Scripture of Hidden Contracts*)[1] written by the *Quanzhen* Daoist Liu Chuxuan 劉處玄 (1147-1203). The *Yinfu jing* is one of the most important Daoist scriptures with a great number of commentaries written by proponents of various Daoist schools still extant in the Daoist Canon today. Liu Chuxuan belongs to the ‚seven perfected' (*qizhen* 七真), the famous group of disciples of the founder of *Quanzhen* 全真 Daoism,[2] Wang Chongyang. *Quanzhen* Daoism emerged in the Jin-dynasty, which the Jurchen established after they had successfully occupied most of northern China and forced the Chinese Song-dynasty to retreat to the south. Today, *Quanzhen* is –along with the *Zhengyi* Daoism of the celestial masters based in Taiwan – one of the two most important branches of Daoism in the Chinese world.

Daoism is not a completely unknown religion in the West anymore. Due to years of arduous scholarship in both the West and in the East, translations of many Daoist scriptures are available even to a greater public in the west. However, our understanding of specific currents and aspects in religious Daoism is remains limited. With this study, I hope to contribute to a better understanding of the nature of religious Daoism.

My study focuses on Liu Chuxuan's commentary. However, the introduction discusses the significance of Daoism and especially the *Quanzhen*-school in contemporary Chinese society and culture. In the first chapter, I discuss the important Daoist context of inner alchemy (*neidan* 內丹) that provides the theoretical framework for Liu Chuxuan's commentary and *Quanzhen* self-cultivation techniques and practices. In the second chapter, I give a historical overview of the emergence of *Quanzhen* Daoism during the Jin-dynasty. This chapter also includes biographical data on Liu Chuxuan available from the Daozang, the Daoist canon and a general discussion of the core concepts used in the teachings of early *Quanzhen* Daoism. The third chapter deals with the *Yinfu jing*, its history and significance in both Daoist

---

1   Hereafter, I use the abbreviated title *Yinfu jing*.
2   *Quanzhen* can be translated as 'ultimate reality' or more literally as 'all-true.' Both translations are common in Western literature. However, because the Chinese word is well-known in the academic world today, I do not give a translation here.

and general Chinese intellectual history. I discuss the still unknown origins of the scripture and give a short overview of other important commentaries on it. In this chapter, I also analyze the controversial role of the classics and 'book learning' in early *Quanzhen* Daoism. The fourth chapter undertakes an interpretation of Liu Chuxuan's commentary. Primarily focusing on general cosmological notions subsumed in the concept of the "Dao of Heaven" and his theory of self-cultivation, I also relate the thoughts expressed in Liu Chuxuan's commentary to texts of other masters of early *Quanzhen* Daoism. I argue that Liu Chuxuan's commentary is an interpretation of Daoist cosmology and theory of inner alchemy that is largely consistent with the thoughts of Wang Chongyang and his other disciples. At the same time however, it displays several features unique to his personality. Finally, the last and central part of this study is the complete and annotated translation of Liu Chuxuan's commentary on the *Yinfu jing*.

Introduction: Daoism in Contemporary China

1. Political perspectives

The Western traveler in contemporary China may have the impression that Daoist religion does not play an important role in daily life anymore. Indeed, one rarely encounters public performances of traditional Daoist rituals, and Daoist temples or monasteries are hardly a ubiquitous sight in the People's Republic of China anymore. In Taiwan, the picture is quite different. Daoist temples dot the landscape, and many people participate in performances and rituals.

The outcome of the Cultural Revolution still affects daily life in the People's Republic of China. During the Cultural Revolution, religion was perceived as superstitious, and the attempt to root out traditional beliefs and ideas resulted in the destruction of many religious sites. However, in the last twenty years religious traditions have been gaining momentum again, and an increasing number of Chinese have started to visit Daoist temples or monasteries. The return of the Daoist religion is echoed in a growing academic interest in Daoism within mainland China.

Due to a major shift in the Communist Party's policies towards religion in the early eighties, many Daoist temples have been restored[1] and the numbers of ordained Daoist priests are growing. The 1982 constitution of the PRC grants religious freedom:

---

1   For a list of all restored Daoist temples see Lai Chi-Tim, *Daoism in China Today, 1980-2002*, in: *The China Quarterly* 2003 174, p.415 fn.10.

> Citizens of the People's Republic of China enjoy freedom of religious belief. No state organ, public organization or individual may compel citizens to believe in any religion: Nor may they discriminate against citizens who believe in, or do not believe in any religion.[2]

Nonetheless, the government's attitude towards religion remains highly ambivalent. While religious activities are permitted in general, many provisions have been made so that they do not escape control. Thus, the article quoted above that grants freedom of religion also delineates guidelines for the regulation of religion by the central government and local administrations:

> The state protects normal religious activities. No one may make use of religion to engage in activities that disrupt public order, impair the health of citizens or interfere with the educational system of the state.[3]

The language used in this article reflects historical experience. Many dynasties of Chinese history were either overthrown by religiously inspired uprisings or greatly affected by emerging religious movements. From the *Yellow Turbans* in the later Han-dynasty to the uprising of the *Taiping* in the 19th century, China's history provides many examples of religious movements *that disrupted public order*. The oppression of the *Falun gong*[4] in recent years shows very well the Chinese government's fear that history might repeat itself yet again.

Governmental control is not restricted to Daoism. All religions practiced in modern China are subject to the surveillance exercised by the Religious Affair's Bureaus of the State Council. This central agency functions as the head to similar institutions in the provinces and major cities.[5] The degree of control exercised varies from region to region and depends on many issues. Generally speaking, however, the Communist Party does not perceive religion as a purely private matter.

In the People's Republic of China, Daoism is organized according to hierarchical principles. The head of religious Daoism in contemporary China is the *National Daoist Association*. The local temples and monasteries usually belong to local Daoist Associations that are organized as subsidiaries of the *National Daoist Association*.

Only two of many Daoist schools have survived in contemporary China: The Daoism of the celestial masters, the *Zhengyi*, and the Daoism of complete perfection,

---

2 Quote taken from Donald E. MacInnis, *Religion in China Today*, New York 1989: Orbis Books, p.34.
3 See ibid.
4 Although this is not the place to discuss this issue, I feel there are many indicators that allow us to classify *falun gong* as a religious movement.
5 See Pitman B. Potter, *Belief in Control: Regulation of Religion in China*, in: *The China Quarterly* 2003.174, p.326-7.

Quanzhen. While both schools are permitted in the People's Republic, the government shows a clear preference for the latter. Most of the restored Daoist monasteries in contemporary China belong to the *Quanzhen* school. While I cannot give a complete and exhaustive explanation of this phenomenon here, an obvious reason needs to be mentioned. *Zhengyi* Daoism, despite its hierarchical structure with the now Taiwan-based celestial master as its spiritual leader, is more likely to escape governmental control. Traditionally, *Zhengyi* Daoism shows a strong tendency towards what in the West would be called laicism. Although traditionally the *daoshi* 道士, or 'priest' of *Zhengyi* Daoism, comprises a profession that must be taught like any other, in contemporary Chinese culture *Zhengyi* Daoists cannot be easily identified. They live their lives as laymen, earn their money with other professions, and, more significantly, no strict hierarchy enables the government to control their religious activities. In contrast, the monastic organization of modern *Quanzhen* Daoism earned it the support of the Communist Party. Most practitioners of this brand of Daoism live in monasteries, which allows the government to exercise control over their religious activities. Furthermore, the headquarters of *Quanzhen* Daoism have never left Mainland China. Ever since the *Yuan*-dynasty, the center of *Quanzhen* Daoism has remained in the *Baiyun guan*, the '*belvedere of the white clouds*' in Beijing.

2. Daoism and Chinese culture

Although based on his research and fieldwork in Taiwan, Kristofer Schipper's general remarks on the nature of Daoism remain valid for both Chinas. He describes Daoism as the "social body of the local communities"[6] and explains the difficulties of applying the Western term 'religion' to Chinese traditions. The Chinese word for religion, *zongjiao* 宗教, literally translates as 'the teachings of the ancestors' and refers to ceremonial aspects of social life. Thus, Daoism cannot be understood from exclusively from its major texts. It is deeply rooted in every day life, in social practices and the consciousness of the Chinese people.

A visit to the *Baiyun guan* 白雲官 in Beijing, the headquarters of the *Quanzhen* school, may give the impression of Daoism's increasing revitalization in contemporary China. The *Baiyun guan* is a temple compound with several halls housing stat-

---

6 Kristofer Schipper, *The Taoist Body*, Taipei 1994: SMC Publishing, p.4.

ues of Daoist deities and immortals. One of the main halls of the compound is devoted to the worship of the *seven perfected* Ma Danyang, Qiu Chuji, Tan Chuduan, Wang Yuyang, Hao Datong, Sun Bu'er and Liu Chuxuan, whose commentary I present in this study. On a typical day, the *Baiyun guan* is not very crowded. However, the stalls of the incense vendors in front of the main gate witness the growing popularity of Daoism in contemporary China. One not only encounters elderly people at the Baiyun guan; even the younger generation of Chinese comes to this place to burn incense and pay their tribute to the deities and immortals. The monks of the *Baiyun guan* stroll around in the compound; sometimes one can encounter them meditating in the temples or practicing divination.

Daoism is certainly the only genuinely Chinese religion. Buddhism and Confucianism both hail from long traditions in China and are deeply rooted in the people's consciousness and daily life. However, it is still debatable whether Confucianism qualifies as a religion at all, and Buddhism is an import from the Indian subcontinent that had to undergo major adjustments before it finally prevailed in China.[7] Daoism on the other hand is *the* Chinese religion. Its basic concepts derived from classical Chinese sources that have influenced both the literati of imperial China and eminent Chinese philosophers. Daoist scriptures themselves have also become part of the broader currents of Chinese intellectual history. The subject of Liu Chuxuan's commentary presented in this paper, exemplifies this mutual influence and penetration of Daoist religion and Chinese culture and philosophy. The *Yinfu jing* was interpreted as a military treatise, and the great neo-Confucian philosopher Zhu Xi wrote one of the most famous and influential commentaries on the scripture. I will say more on this point in the third chapter of my study.

The history of religious Daoism is the history of both practice and literature. In its thousands of years of vibrant development, Daoism has produced an unparalleled multitude of texts. Many but not all have been collected in the *Zhengtong Daozang*, the Daoist canon. In contemporary China, we notice a growing interest in the legacy of religious Daoism. A number of scholars write on different aspects of Daoism, but more important the *Quanzhen*-monks of the *Baiyun guan* in Beijing are preparing a new punctuated edition of the Daoist Canon that will be published in the near future.[8] The Daoist canon not only attracts the interest of faithful followers of religious

---

7 It must be mentioned here that the so-called 'three teachings' Buddhism, Daoism and Confucianism have always influenced each other. Later in this study, we will see that 'the unification of the three teachings' was an integral part of early *Quanzhen* Daoism.
8 Professor Florian C. Reiter of the Humboldt University has told me about this major endeavor.

Daoism or scholars of religious traditions. It also provides access to China's social history and the intellectual development of Chinese culture. Many famous Daoists were also outstanding writers, and especially the founder of *Quanzhen* Daoism, Wang Chongyang, and his seven disciples left sizable collections of poetry. Many of these are still available in the Daoist Canon.

For a long time, the patriarchs of early *Quanzhen* Daoism have been very popular figures in vernacular literature. The Ming-dynasty novel *Qizhen zhuan* (*Tale of the Seven Perfected*) epitomizes this popularity. This novel narrates a largely fictitious version of the emergence of *Quanzhen* Daoism, the early days of the 'missionary work' of the *seven perfected* and their self-cultivation. One chapter tells the story of Liu Chuxuan who stays in a brothel in order to confront and eventually dissolve his sexual desires. The anonymous author of the novel writes about Liu Chuxuan's demeanor in the brothel:

> Madam Yü looked at Liu Ch'ang-sheng and saw that he was not only handsome, but had a regal bearing that set him apart from other customers. Whereas her other customers desired her body and often made violent sexual approaches to her, this man respected her and spoke to her gently, treating her not as a sexual object but as a friend. Liu Ch'ang-sheng conducted himself according to what Wang Ch'ung-yang had taught him: "View everything before you with calmness. True stillness is when a landslide passes before you and you are not disturbed." Thus, Liu Ch'ang-sheng treated the beautiful woman before him as an empty form. His heart was not moved, and therefore his body did not desire her.[9]

This quote shows that the anonymous author must have possessed a profound knowledge of *Quanzhen* Daoism. The last sentence echoes motifs of *Quanzhen* also found in Liu Chuxuan's commentary on the *Yinfu jing*.

While this novel is certainly not very popular anymore in contemporary China or Taiwan, the story told in it still has great appeal to many Chinese. One of the most popular kung fu novels, the *Shendiao xialüe*, takes place during the Jin-dynasty and describes the main character's fight against the foreign occupation. The central character received his education and martial arts training from *Quanzhen* masters. Although the story is an imaginary tale not based on any historical sources, it demonstrates the appeal of early *Quanzhen* Daoism for a broader audience in contemporary China. This novel enjoys such great popularity that it has even inspired a very successful series of comic books, as well as a movie based on the story. The history of early *Quanzhen* Daoism has also influenced another noteworthy aspect of contempo-

---

9   Eva Wong (transl.), *Seven Taoist Masters. A Folk Novel of China*, Boston 1990: Shambhala Publications Inc., p.115.

rary Chinese popular culture. Fantasy role-playing games enjoy enormous popularity among the younger generation of Chinese. These games are usually based on pseudo-historic scenarios found in kung fu novels. Some of the most popular characters used in these games are Wang Chongyang and his seven disciples. The characters are endowed with mystical powers similar to those acquired by the historical 'seven perfected' according to the hagiographical material found in the *Daoist canon*.

However, I do not want to imply that *Quanzhen* possesses an exclusively imaginary nature today, only alive in the minds of artists and writers. Despite the more obviously religious activities in Daoist monasteries or temples, the most significant influences of Daoist traditions in contemporary China can be found in the modern practices of *qigong* or *taiji quan*. These exercises depart from the Daoist traditions of 'nurturing life'[10] based on the assumption that a rigorous self-cultivation leads to longevity and ultimately immortality.[11] While the numerous schools of Daoism have each produced unique and distinct approaches to the central goal of this religion, the basic themes have always remained unchanged. The different theories, techniques and practices are subsumed in a term that translates as '*the art of immortality.*'[12] The most influential theories and practices belonging to this tradition are the ancient *qigong*, the outer and the inner alchemy. Despite great differences between these theories, they all share some basic concepts and assumptions and make use of the same classical scriptures and texts.

The central concern in religious Daoism – and *Quanzhen* certainly makes no exception here – is the attainment of longevity and ultimately immortality.[13] The *Quanzhen* Daoist believes that a rigorous self-cultivation will extend one's lifespan and eventually lead to immortality, which may not necessarily be understood as a physical but as a different kind of existence.[14] I will argue that *Quanzhen* focuses on

---

10 Chin. *yang sheng* 養生

11 See Li Yuanguo, *Daojiao qigong yangsheng xue*, Chengdu 1988: Sichuan sheng shehui kexueyuan chubanshe, p.47: "Religious Daoism focuses on cultivation and nurturing. 'Cultivation' is related to 'cultivating the essence' and 'cultivating the *qi*.' 'Nurturing' is related to 'nurturing being' and 'nurturing the spirits.' This is also called 'practicing quiescence.' By passing through a firmly based practice of cultivation, they [the Daoists] hope to attain an extended lifespan, an elongated existence and even reach the wonderland of eternal life."

12 Chin. *xianshu* 仙術, ibid.

13 For a general introduction to Daoism focusing on these issues see: John Blofeld, *Taoism – the Quest for Immortality*, London 1979: Allen & Unwin.

14 See Holmes Welsh, *The Parting of the Way*, USA 1966: The Beacon Press, p. 131 on the embryonic self that is the eventual outcome of inner alchemy and not *physically* immortal.

these issues, both relying on more ancient traditions and inventing new approaches to an unchanged theme.

In short, religious Daoism is not only alive in contemporary China and Taiwan, its underlying theory, its main concepts and ideas permeate everyday life. Daoism is so deeply rooted in Chinese culture that the application of a Western concept of religion is out of place here. Even someone who does not consider himself a follower of Daoism may practice gymnastics or techniques deriving from the Daoist legacies of *neidan* (*inner alchemy*) or *yangsheng* (*nurturing life*). In doing so, they apply concepts that may at least partially derive from discourses shaped by the protagonists of early *Quanzhen*.

1

Inner Alchemy (neidan 內丹)

1. The term *inner alchemy*

While some scholars have tried to distill a coherent theory of *inner alchemy* (*neidan* 內丹) from the existing sources,[1] the texts and practices associated with this term are extremely heterogeneous. In essence, the term applies to a body of texts in- and outside the Daoist canon, as well as the mental and physical practices described in those texts.[2] This rich tradition provides the context and theoretical framework for Liu Chuxuan's commentary on the *Yinfu jing* and other self-cultivation texts ascribed to the protagonists of early *Quanzhen* Daoism. Hence, without an introduction to some of the basic concepts and ideas of *inner alchemy*, many aspects of Liu Chuxuan's theory of self-cultivation as outlined in his commentary would remain opaque.

From my point of view, a general theory of *inner alchemy* remains doomed as an ahistorical project that fails to take the peculiarities of specific authors into account. *Inner alchemy* confronts readers who are unfamiliar with Daoist literature with an extremely codified symbolic language. Moreover, every author interprets this symbolic language in a unique way. The author's personal background, affiliation with a

---

1 The most outstanding example of this approach can be found in Needham's *History of Science and Civilisation in China*. See Joseph Needham and Lu Gwei-Djen, *Science and Civilisation in China. Vol. 5: Chemistry and Chemical Technology. Part V: Spagyrical Discovery and Invention: Physiological Alchemy*. Taibei 1986 (repr.): Caves Books.

2 See Fabrizio Pregadio and Lowell Skar, *Inner Alchemy (Neidan)*, in: Livia Kohn (ed.), *Daoism Handbook*, Leiden, Boston, Köln 2000: Brill, p.464-65.

specific school of Daoist thought, and scholarly ambitions may all contribute to his reading of inner alchemy symbols. In order to provide the reader with a broader understanding of Liu Chuxuan's commentary, I explore this background in the other chapters of this study.

Despite the heterogeneous nature of *inner alchemy*, most texts in this tradition share some common features. In this chapter, I give a short introduction to the meaning of the term *inner alchemy* (*neidan*) itself and explain some of its central concepts, which are largely related to basic principles of Daoist cosmology. In doing so, I rely mainly on the extensive secondary literature on this part of the Daoist legacy that is still available today. When drawing on primary sources, I make use of the writings of Wang Chongyang's seven disciples and the writings of Wang Chongyang himself.

As Farzeen Baldrian-Hussein points out, the origin of the term *inner alchemy* (*neidan*) is difficult to determine.[3] Baldrian-Hussein shows that the term *neidan* does not appear in sources written before the Tang (618-907) and the Song-dynasty (960-1279). However, even in the texts from these periods associated with inner alchemy the term itself does not appear very often.

Today, *inner alchemy* or *neidan* generally refers to a set of physiological and mental exercises aimed at the extension of the practitioner's lifespan.[4] The ultimate goal of these exercises or techniques lies in the attainment of immortality. This is also the genuinely Daoist feature of inner alchemy because immortality has always constituted the central theme in religious Daoism. Some of the techniques and practices associated with *inner alchemy* are themselves more ancient than the comparatively new term that signifies them. As such, *inner alchemy* was not a revolutionary invention. It was based on traditions probably stretching back to the times of the two Daoist classics *Daode jing* 道德經 and *Zhuangzi* 壯子. Key terms such as Dao, the 'void' or 'non-being,' originate from these classical scriptures.[5]

What was new about *inner alchemy* when it emerged, however, was its attempt to organize diverse practices into a codified system and "*give greater weight to intellectual speculation of an original and unique form.*"[6] As mentioned above, this did not yield a single, unified tradition, but rather a multitude of new traditions based on

---

3 See Farzeen Baldrian-Hussein, *Inner Alchemy: Notes on the Origin and Use of the Term Neidan*, in: Cahiers d'Extreme-Asie. 1989: Vol. 5, p.165-69.
4 See Paulino T. Belamide, *Self-Cultivation and Quanzhen Daoism with special Reference to the Legacy of Qiu Chuji*, UMI 2002, p.76.
5 Chin. *dao* 道, *xu* 虛 and *wu* 無. See ibid., p.80.
6 Isabelle Robinet, *Original Contributions of Neidan to Taoism and Chinese Thought*, in: Livia Kohn (ed.), *Taoist Meditation and Longevity Techniques*, Ann Arbor 1989: The University of Michigan Press, p.299.

the same corpus of texts. In the times of the Jin-dynasty (1115-1234), *Quanzhen* Daoism established one of these new traditions, which today remains the most important in China.

Neidan is commonly translated as 'inner elixir.' Hence, it is quite literally the terminological opposite of *waidan* 外丹, the 'outer elixir' or the 'outer alchemy.' The outer alchemy displays certain similarities to European alchemical traditions.[7] In proto-chemical processes, the practitioner of outer alchemy tried to amalgamate a 'golden pill' or the 'drug of immortality.'[8] While texts belonging to the current of *inner alchemy* use a similar or sometimes identical proto-chemical language, the processes of refinement they describe are quite different. In the worldview of *inner alchemy* the human body comprises 'the laboratory' used for alchemical processes of refinement.

2. The theory of reversion

In inner alchemy, the main "ingredients" are the same as in *outer alchemy*: Lead and mercury. However, whereas *outer alchemy* refers to material substance when using those terms, in *inner alchemy* they are primarily symbolic.[9] When *inner alchemy* furnishes alchemical terminology, this terminology applies to the human body. Lead and mercury designate physiological entities that are present in the human body. The goal of *inner alchemy* is a thorough transformation of the substances contained in the human body and thus a transformation of the complete human being.

This transformation should not be misunderstood as a progressive development however. In fact, the inner alchemist attempts to reverse the normal process of nature or creation and return to a primordial state of being. Unlike outer alchemy, *inner alchemy* does not aspire to produce a new and formerly inexistent substance. Not only are the ingredients already present in the human body, but the refined state of being that the 'perfected man' of *Quanzhen* represents also belongs to the past, not the fu-

---

7 See Mircea Eliade, *Yoga, Immortality and Freedom*, New York 1958: Pantheon Books, pp. 284-290.
8 Chin. *jindan* 金丹 and *xianyao* 仙藥.
9 DZ 1158 *Chongyang zhenren shou danyang ershisi jue*, 1b, provides the following explanation: "Lead, that is the original spirit. Mercury, that is the original *qi*. Their names are lead and mercury." For the terms spirit and *qi* see the third section of this chapter.

ture. *Inner alchemy* is 'positively' regressive, targeted at a former and more perfected state of being. In the language employed in the texts of *inner alchemy*, this positive regression finds its expression in the antinomy of "walking forward" (*shunxing* 順行) and "walking reverse" (*nixing* 逆行). While the worldly people follow the cosmological processes that ultimately lead to decay and death, the immortals or *perfected men* of inner alchemy reverse those processes. In Liu Chuxuan's worldview these two patterns of behavior reflect man's ability to exist in accordance with celestial principles:

> Those who follow the will of Heaven go against [the normal course of nature]; those who act against the will of Heaven follow [the normal course of nature].

天意順者逆行，逆者順行。[10]

The theory of reversion to a former and perfected state of being as described in the texts of inner alchemy is based on cosmological principles that make up the fundaments of Daoist thought in general. But inner alchemy goes beyond more ancient traditions of Daoist self-cultivation by integrating cosmological concepts into an esoteric and highly complex philosophical system that draws on the theory of changes outlined in the ancient *Yijing* 易經 and its many commentaries; the Daoist classic *Zhouyi cantong qi* 周易參同契, ascribed to the legendary Han-dynasty immortal Wei Boyang 魏伯陽; and the theory of the five phases or elements, which is fundamental to Chinese philosophical speculation in general.

The most fundamental cosmological principle used in inner alchemy is the distinction between a state called "anterior Heaven" (*xiantian* 先天) and a state called "posterior Heaven" (*houtian* 後天). As is the case with many concepts in Chinese thought, these two symbolic expressions are not complete opposites, but instead complement one another. One term would not exist without the other. And while the natural process of creation inevitably leads from anterior to posterior Heaven, from birth to death, from blooming to wilting, a reversion of this process is never excluded in principle. The goal of inner alchemy thus represents an almost necessary outcome of Chinese cosmological speculations. Originally macrocosmic principles, in *inner alchemy* the two states "anterior Heaven" and "posterior Heaven" signify cosmological principles that are mirrored in the microcosmic processes of the human body.

---

10 DZ 122, 15b.

In *inner alchemy* the cosmological patterns of the states "anterior Heaven" and "posterior Heaven" are represented in two different configurations of the trigrams from the *Yijing*:

> In the first configuration, which represents the unconditioned state "before Heaven", original yin and yang are represented by the trigrams *kun* ☷ at due North and *qian* ☰ at due South, respectively, while *li* ☲ and *kan* ☵ are at due East and West, respectively. In the configuration related to the state "after Heaven", *qian* and *kun* are displaced to other positions, and their places are taken by *kan* (North) and *li* (South). In other words, *kan* is the conditioned aspect of *kun*, and *li* is the conditioned aspect of *qian*.[11]

The representations of the two configurations associated with "anterior Heaven" and "posterior Heaven" and their use in the theory of both *outer* and *inner alchemy* depart from the ancient text *Zhouyi cantong qi*. In its opening paragraph, the *Zhouyi cantongqi* says:

> As for *qian* and *kun*, they are the opening gates to change, and they are mother and father to all trigrams. *Kan* and *li* are the frames and the rims, the correct axis of the revolving hub.

乾坤者，易之門戶，眾卦之父母。坎離匡廓，運轂正軸。[12]

The trigram *qian* consists of three unbroken *Yang*-lines, whereas the trigram *kun* has three broken *Yin*-lines. *Kan*, however, contains one unbroken *Yang*-line inside of two broken *Yin*-lines, and *li* has a broken *yin*-line enclosed by two unbroken *Yang*-lines. In *Inner alchemy*, the unbroken *Yang*-line in the center of *kan* is known as *Real Fire*,[13] the broken *Yin*-line in the center of *li* known as *Real Water*.[14] In the cosmological processes that lead to *posterior Heaven*, the two trigrams *kan* and *li* were created by interchanging the central lines of *qian* and *kun*.

Inner alchemy strove to 're-create' the trigrams *qian* and *kun*[15] and restore them to their former place in the configuration associated with the primordial state of anterior Heaven by returning *Real Fire* and *Real Water* to their original positions in the trigrams *qian* and *kun*.[16] In doing so, the 'natural' flow of things in the cosmological

---

11 Fabrizio Pregadio and Lowell Skar 2000, p.483.
12 DZ 1008 *Zhouyi cantong qi*, 1.1a. For a more exhaustive survey of the use of the trigrams in the *Zhouyi cantong qi* please consult Fabrizio Pregadio, *The Representation of Time in the Zhouyi cantong qi*, in: Cahiers d´Extreme-Asie 1995, vol. 8, p.155-173.
13 Chin. *zhenhuo* 真火.
14 Chin. *zhenshui* 真水.
15 See Joseph Needham and Lu Gwei-Djen 1986, p.42.
16 The *inner alchemy* technique associated with this theory was named 'Taking from *kan* and

state posterior Heaven would be reversed. *Yin* would sink down to earth in the state of posterior Heaven and *Yang* would rise to Heaven. These two contrary movements of the fundamental cosmological principles *Yin* and *Yang* lead to the formation of Heaven and Earth, but eventually also to death and decay. When those movements are reversed, man escapes his fate and achieves immortality. In *inner alchemy*, the hexagram *tai* from the *Yijing* symbolizes the completion of the desired reversion to and restoration of the primordial state in which *Yang* descends and *Yin* rises. The hexagram *tai* 泰 contains the trigrams *kun* on the top and *kan* on the bottom. Liu Chuxuan's *Yinfu jing* commentary contains the following passage:

> The correct Dao has the radiance of the sun and the moon. Even when the night is dark and the radiance is feeble, it is still revealing like the radiance of the sun and the moon. It plainly illuminates the ten directions and the three realms. Is this like seeing the light of a firefly? The saints grasp the universe, Yin and Yang mutate thoroughly, and Heaven and Earth unite in Peace (*tai*).

> 正道有似日月之光。夜暗則微光且顯若見日月之光。耀照偏十方三界。豈見螢耀也。聖人掌握宇宙，陰陽通變，地天交泰。[17]

In the text *Anthology of Taigu*, Hao Datong gives an explanation of the significance of the phrase "Heaven and Earth unite in peace (*tai*)":

> The *Yang-qi* of Heaven descends into Earth, and the *Yin-qi* of Earth rises to Heaven above. This is called "Heaven and Earth unite" and they form [the hexagram] *tai*.

> 天之陽氣下降地中、地之陰氣升而天上。此謂天地交而成太。[18]

In the terminology of *inner alchemy*, the wisdom of the saints lies in their ability to make Heaven and Earth unite. The hexagram *tai* symbolizes this return to the primordial state of *anterior Heaven* through the reciprocal change of positions of the *Yang*-trigram *qian* and the *Yin*-trigram *kun*.

    The theory of *inner alchemy* combines the principle of reversion that I outlined above with the traditional Chinese concept of the five elements or agents[19] wood, metal, fire, earth and water. While the theory of reversion from *posterior Heaven* to *anterior Heaven* derives from the application of cosmological principles, the theory

---

    filling in *li'*(*qukan tianli shu* 取坎填離術). For a thorough exploration of the theory and the technique see: Paulino Belamide 2002, p.94-97.

17 DZ 122, 3a.
18 DZ 1161 *Taigu ji* 太古集, 2.3b.
19 Chin. *wuxing* 五行.

of the five elements describes the processes at stake in the natural world of physical reality. The interactions of the five elements bring forth all beings and inform both the human body and mind. Hence, the theory of the five elements epitomizes the traditional Chinese identification of macrocosmic and microcosmic structures and processes.[20]

In traditional Chinese thought, the five elements appear in several non-accidental cyclical orders. The most relevant order here is the 'productive' order, which describes the cyclical production of the elements or agents. The Han-dynasty Confucian philosopher Dong Zhongshu describes the cyclical production of the elements in the following fashion:

> Heaven comprises five elements: the first is wood, the second fire, the third earth, the fourth metal and the fifth water. Wood is the beginning of the cycle, water the last, and earth is in the center of the circle. Such is the order given by nature. Wood produces fire, fire produces earth, earth metal, metal water, water wood. This is the faher-son relationship.[21]

In inner alchemy, the central goal of a complete reversion of the natural creational processes also applies to the representation of the five elements, this reversion is known as "toppling the five elements."[22] The techniques of self-cultivation practiced by the followers of *Quanzhen* and other Daoist schools were believed to bring forth a new order of the five elements that would result in a process contrary to the natural processes symbolized in the natural order Dong Zhongshu described. The natural productive cycle functions according to the principles of *posterior Heaven* that are – as I argued above - the reasons for decay and death. When reversed, the cyclical order of the five elements would lead back to its origin and a practitioner of self-cultivation would move from death to birth, contrary to the natural flow. In other words, the theory of "toppling the five elements" expresses the same basic notions as the theory of reversion outlined in the *Zhouyi cantong qi*. Both are integrated into the body of *inner alchemy*. Together, they provide the theoretical back-

---

20 In his commentary on the *Yinfu jing* (DZ 122, 6b), Liu Chuxuan provides a good example for the application of the five elements in an *inner alchemy* context: "Fire gives birth to the human mind. It happens daily and everywhere. The unchanging evil lies in wood, and thus it becomes the inner nature of man. If one's thoughts are not enlightened, the fire ignites the inner nature, which is [made of the element] wood."
21 This quote is taken from Chang Chung-yang, *Creativity and Taoism*, New York 1963: The Julian Press, p. 139.
22 *Wuxing diandao* 五行顛倒. This term appears in DZ 122, 2b.

ground for the elaborate descriptions of specific techniques of self-cultivation contained in the texts associated with *inner alchemy*.

3. Practice: The three treasures and the restoration of primordial *Yang-qi*

In *inner alchemy*, the three main substances of the alchemical process are known as the 'three treasures.'[23] These three treasures are essence, spirit and *qi*.[24] In the text DZ 1057 *Chongyang zhenren shou danyang ershisi jue* (Twenty-four Instructions the Perfected Man Chongyang Bestowed on Danyang), Wang Chongyang answers Ma Danyang's question about the three treasures:

> There are three outer and three inner treasures. The Dao, the Classics and the masters constitute the three outer treasures. As for the three inner treasures, they are essence, *qi* and spirit."[25]

23　Chin. *sanbao*三寶. This term was probably coined from a Buddhist term. See Paulino T. Belamide, *Self Cultivation and Quanzhen Daoism with special Reference to the Legacy of Qiu Chuji*, UMI Dissertation Services 2002, p.83.

24　In Chinese, the three treasures are called *jing*精, *shen*神 and *qi*氣. Literally, *jing* denotes the male semen; it is a substance residing in the kidneys. Commonly, it is translated as essence. The literal meaning of *shen* is spirit; and in inner alchemy and other Daoist contexts, it refers to the spiritual aspects of the complete human being. Thus, a literal translation as spirit is most suitable here. *Qi*, however, is a very complex term with multiple connotations and with no immediate equivalent in any Western language. Many scholars use the literal meaning of *qi* as a translation: Breath. I do not follow this common practice in my translation because Liu Chuxuan uses the term in at least two different ways. On the one hand, *qi* appears as an all-permeating energy that informs all beings. On the other hand, *qi* is also used for the winds of the celestial directions. In Daoist thought, these two different meanings do not necessarily have to be distinguished. Thus, I have opted to leave the term untranslated and provide explanatory footnotes where necessary. See also: Ute Engelhardt, *Die klassische Tradition der Qi-Übungen (Qigong): Eine Darstellung anhand des Tang-zeitlichen Textes Fuqi jingyi lun von Sima Chengzhen*. Stuttgart 1987: Franz Steiner Verlag Wiesbaden GmbH, p.1-6.

25　I will not analyze the distinction between outer and inner treasures here. The distinction refers to an important topic in early *Quanzhen* Daoism that I will discuss in depth in the

有外內三寶。是道經師者爲外三寶也。內三寶者，精氣神也。[26]

Together, the three inner treasures constitute the complete physical and mental human being represented in the writings of inner alchemists. The practices circumscribed in the symbolic language of inner alchemy texts aim at the transformation of these 'treasures.'

While the five elements and the trigrams *qian* and *kun*, *li* and *kan* play an important role for the more theoretical aspects of *inner alchemy*, the practices described in the texts focus on the refinement of essence, spirit and *qi*. The three treasures are believed to occupy three distinct spaces in the body. In Daoism, these spaces are also known as the lower, the central and the upper cinnabar-fields.[27] In traditional Daoist meditations, the adept practitioner tries to focus his imagination on these fields in order to refine the three treasures associated with them.

Among the three treasures, *qi* performs a unique role. *Qi* is a ubiquitous energy, present not only in the human body, but also in all beings. In different manifestations, it has always been present, from the pre-creational state of *anterior Heaven* to the state of *posterior Heaven*. According to Daoist cosmology, the *qi* was originally one but subsequently split to form Heaven, Earth and eventually the ten thousand things. The foreword to the *Quanzhen*-cultivation text *Straightforward Instructions on the Great Elixir* (*Dadan zhizhi*) attributed to Qiu Chuji[28] describes this part of Daoist cosmology in detail:

> Heaven and Earth are originally one *qi* of the great void. When stillness is at its utmost [moment], it moves and transforms into two. The light rises up and becomes *Yang* and Heaven; the heavy and turbid sinks down and becomes *Yin* and Earth. They are split into two, yet they cannot [remain] still. Because the *qi* of Heaven moves and descends in order to unite with the *qi* of Earth, it ascends again once it reaches the [lowest] extreme. [...] [The *qi*] above and [the *qi*] below need each other – and their change gives birth to the ten thousand things.

---

second chapter of this study.

26 DZ 1057, 2a.

27 The lower cinnabar-field is located in the area of the navel or the abdomen. The central cinnabar-field designates the heart, and the upper cinnabar-field is located behind the forehead. Hence, in *inner alchemy* the spatial distinction of the three treasures is much more important than any substantial difference between them. See DZ 244 *Dadan zhizhi* 大丹直指, 3a: "The lower cinnabar [field] is the place of essence. The central cinnabar [field] is the courtyard of *qi*. The upper cinnabar [field] is the temple of the spirit."

28 The historical value of this text is disputable. It was probably not written by *Qiu Chuji* himself but compiled by his disciples. However as a source of early *Quanzhen* cultivation practices and the theory of *inner alchemy* in general, the text is very important and useful.

天地本太空一氣靜極則動變而為二。輕清向上，為陽為天，動濁向下，為陰為地。既分而為二，亦不能靜。因天氣先動，降下以合地氣至極復升。（・・・）上下相須不已，化生萬物。²⁹

From a cosmological point of view, Yin and Yang are essentially the one primordial *qi*; in productive cycles, this primordial *qi* moves from an undifferentiated state of Oneness through increasingly differentiated and complex states. In doing so, it produces the phenomenal world and ultimately leads to decay and death. Within the worldview of inner alchemy, the human body forms a microcosm that mimics these macrocosmic productive cycles from birth to death:

> Man and Heaven and Earth all receive the One, and they share the same origin. Because of the union of the two *qi* of father and mother, [the two *qi*] mix and merge, and they become the 'pearl'. Within it, a dot of the *perfect qi* of primordial *Yang* is stored.

人與天地受一同始因父母二氣交感混合成珠內藏一點元陽真氣。³⁰

In the microcosmic reality of human existence, the pre-natal state of the fetus in the mother's womb parallels the macrocosmic primordial state of *anterior Heaven*. The fetus stores primordial *Yang-qi*. But as soon as the fetus is born, a gradual decay sets in. In the worldview of *inner alchemy*, the natural process that leads to death is equated with a gradual exhaustion of the primordial *Yang* that the fetus is endowed with when it is born. Death occurs when the entire primordial *Yang* of the newborn child has been exhausted. The techniques and practices of *inner alchemy* therefore focus on the restoring of primordial *Yang-qi* and preventing a terminal exhaustion of this energy.

However, in *Quanzhen* Daoism, the theory of *inner alchemy* did not produce a coherent and codified methodology of practices. Instead, practice remained an individual affair and depended greatly on the unique personalities of the student and his preferences. Thus, the practices of each of the proponents of early *Quanzhen Daoism* displayed unique features. In DZ 1056 *Jinzhenren* yulu, Ma Danyang comments on the "the *regulation of breath*," a central practice of *inner alchemy*. He explains that this practice in *Quanzhen inner alchemy* is not based on conscious and learned behavior:³¹

---

29 DZ 244, 1.1a.
30 Ibid., 1.1b.
31 See Florian C. Reiter, *Grundelemente und Tendenzen des Religiösen Taoismus*, Wiesbaden 1988, p.74. Reiter gives a German translation of this passage.

Someone asked what the 'regulation of breath' was. He (Ma Danyang) answered: "There is no (learned) activity. When there are no [worldly] matters in the mind, the breath of *qi* regulates itself. Only then one knows that the regulation of breath is achieved. The regulation of breath can only be achieved unknowingly. It cannot be actively pursued through [a regulation of] mouth and nose."

問如何調息。答曰非有作也。若得心中無事氣息自調。但知調息便是有著。調息者只可不知見。不可著於口鼻。[32]

Hence, the self-cultivation texts ascribed to masters of early *Quanzhen* Daoism do not provide the reader with a detailed description of practices or techniques. From Ma Danyang's point of view, no theoretical description could help understanding and applying a method that indeed is based on the idea of a return to a completely unconscious attitude. A follower of *Quanzhen* could only gain access to the proper ways of self-cultivation by personal training through a spiritual master and an individual and intuitive practice.[33] More importantly, the follower of *Quanzhen* must first experience enlightenment in the fashion of Liu Chuxuan's enlightenment, which will be described in the next chapter. In most hagiographies of *Quanzhen* masters, this enlightenment is of a sudden nature, sometimes just triggered by the encounter with Wang Chongyang or by certain mysterious incidents that exceed the realm of the normal. This enlightenment eventually produces a completely altered mind and provides the basis for further practices as delineated in Liu Chuxuan's commentary that would not be accessible to the unenlightened and ignorant man.

---

32 DZ 1056 *Jinzhenren yulu* 晉真人語錄, 7b.
33 Although I will argue that Liu Chuxuan's commentary should be read as a didactic book, it does not give any instructions on specific techniques. Only the devout student of a Quanzhen master would be able to grasp the complete meaning of its symbolic language and apply it in his Daoist meditations.

2

Liu Chuxuan and Early *Quanzhen*-Daoism

1. The emergence of early *Quanzhen*-Daoism

As I argued in the introduction to this study, *Quanzhen* comprises one of the two most important schools in contemporary religious Daoism. Its most outstanding feature is a monastic and hierarchical structure that gives it an outlook very different from the other important brand of Daoism, the school of the celestial masters called *Zhengyi*. However, when *Quanzhen* emerged it was less predictable whether it would eventually develop in this fashion. In fact, one of the unique characteristics of early *Quanzhen* Daoism was its individualistic approach to the themes of religious Daoism. The path towards immortality and sainthood described in the writings of its founder Wang Chongyang and of his seven disciples, the so-called seven perfected, was a very personal affair.[1]

In this chapter, I will provide a short introduction to the early history of *Quanzhen*-Daoism. I situate the narratives of Wang Chongyang's founding of *Quanzhen* and Liu Chuxuan's encounter with the school in the historical context of 12th century China. These narratives are based on the hagiographical data found in the Daoist Canon. The hagiographies are not primarily interesting for their historic accuracy, but most intriguing here for their attempt to re-interpret the lives of the protagonists of early *Quanzhen* Daoism in light of *Quanzhen*-teachings. Hence, I

---

[1] For an account of the history of *Quanzhen* Daoism until the times of the Yuan-dynasty see Paul Demiéville, *La Situation Religieuse en Chine au Temps de Marco Polo*, in: Oriente Poliano 1957, p.197 – 201.

discuss the basic concepts and beliefs of *Quanzhen* after my historic overview of the school. My exploration illustrates that the lives of Wang Chongyang and Liu Chuxuan as discussed in the hagiographies both represent an individual existence that accords with *Quanzhen* teachings.

When *Quanzhen* emerged during the 12th century, China was divided into a northern and a southern part. The Jin dynasty, established by the alien nomadic people of the Jurchen, governed the north, while the Song dynasty, which had previously ruled China in its entirety, continued to govern as the southern Song in the region south of the Jiangzi. During the previous decades, China had witnessed a period of ceaseless war and conflict between the Jurchen and Song. The outcome of this period was not only the permanent division of China, but more important, and certainly more humiliating in the minds of Chinese intellectuals, a defeated Chinese dynasty that had to pay tribute to an alien regime in the North.[2] The division of China had an impact on religious history as well.[3] Due to decreasing contacts between the North and the South, religious Daoism developed quite differently in the two regions. As to inner alchemy, two major schools gained currency: Wang Chongyang's school in the North and a Southern school established by the famous Zhang Boduan.[4] Later, both schools would be integrated into one.

Along with the Daoist schools of *Taiyi* 太一 and *Dadao* 大道, *Quanzhen* is known as one of the three "new Daoist schools."[5] These three schools emerged around the same time in northern China, and to some extent, were all reactions to the unusual situation of a politically divided China with an alien regime in the North. In many ways, all three schools marked a departure from the teachings of the traditional *Zhengyi*-Daoism of the celestial masters because they stressed the significance of individual self-cultivation. But there are important differences between them. While both the *Taiyi* and the *Dadao* disappeared after a comparatively short period of time, *Quanzhen* has continued to flourish to this day. But another striking feature

---

2   For a historical overview of the Jin dynasty see Herbert Franke, *The Chin dynasty*, in: Herbert Franke and Denis Twitchett (eds.), *The Cambridge History of China. Vol. 6: Alien Regimes and Border States, 907-1368*, Cambridge 1984: Cambridge University Press, p.215-320.
3   See ibid., p.313 and T'ao-chung Yao, *Buddhism and Taoism under the Chin*, in: Hoyt Cleveland Tillman and Stephen H. West (eds.), *China under Jurchen Rule. Essays on Chin Intellectual and Cultural History*, Albany 1995: State University of New York Press, p.145-180.
4   For a short description of Zhang Boduan's theory of alchemy see Holmes Welch, *Taoism: The Parting of the Way*, 1966, p.131.
5   Guo Zhan, *Quanzhendao de xingqi yu jinwangchao de guanxi*, in: SJZYJ, 3/1983, p.99.

sets *Quanzhen* apart from the two other schools that took shape in the 12th century. While the Daoist Canon preserved an extensive body of texts associated with the protagonists of early *Quanzhen*, *Taiyi* and *Dadao* left behind almost no texts that might provide a deeper knowledge of their teachings.[6]

Like his seven disciples, Wang Chongyang was raised in a wealthy family. He was born in the village *Dawei* 大魏 located in the *Xianyang* 咸陽 district of Shaanxi. He enjoyed a traditional education in classical Chinese literature and later joined the academy in *Jingzhao* 京兆. However, he did not pursue a career as a mandarin, which was customary for a member of the Chinese gentry, but instead became a soldier. After successfully passing the military exams, he changed his personal name to *Dewei* 德威 ("virtuous strength") and his style to *Shixiong* 世雄 ("Hero of a generation"), probably in order to express his determination. Later, he would discover that the life of a soldier could not satisfy his needs and aspirations.[7] At age 47, he abandoned his military career, left his family and retreated from social life.

He took up residence in the small village of *Liujiang* 劉蔣 in the *Zhongnan* 終南 district, where he lived in a small hut. According to legend, he was caught drunk in the streets many times, but about a year after his retreat from society, he encountered two immortals in a butcher shop located in the nearby village of *Ganhe* 甘河.[8] In the hagiographies of the Daoist Canon, this encounter marks the beginning of Wang Chongyang's path towards enlightenment and immortality. Shortly after this encounter, Wang changed his name again. He took *Zhe* 喆 as his personal name and *Zhiming* 知明 ("He who knows about clarity") as his style. At the same time, he took the Daoist name *Chongyang* 重陽 ("Double Yang"), by which he is still known today. The choice of these names indicates Wang's determination to change his life and start searching for spiritual enlightenment and his aspiration to become a Daoist sage.

Among the other supernatural encounters narrated in the hagiographies, one stands out in particular. In 1164, Wang met a Daoist master who introduced himself as the famous Liu Haichan. Liu let Wang fetch water from a nearby river and drink it. Wang was surprised to discover that the water had instantly turned into the "wine of

---

6   For an exhaustive account of the surviving literary anthologies attributed to the masters of early Quanzhen Daoism see Judith Boltz, *A Survey of Taoist Literature, Tenth to Seventeenth Century*, Berkeley 1987, p. 142 – 166.

7   At age 47, Wang sighed: "At age 40, Kongzi was without any doubts. And when Mengzi was 40, his mind was resting in itself. And I am still doing this hard work? Is this not stupidity?" See *Lishi zhenxian tidao tongjian xupian*, 1.1b – 1.2a.

8   Ibid.

the immortals."⁹ The story is important because abstinence from alcohol and other vices became a central issue in Wang's later teachings. After this incident, Wang never drank any wine again.¹⁰ Shortly after this encounter with Liu Haichan, Wang burned down his hut, dancing and singing ecstatically. Allegedly, he also said: "In three years someone will come and re-build this hut."¹¹

Wang Chongyang traveled to Shandong where he began to spread his teachings. At first, these did not have a great impact on the general public, but they did attract the interest of Shandong's educated elite. Wang's famous seven disciples - Ma Danyang, Sun Bu'er, Qiu Chuji, Tan Chuduan, Hao Datong and Liu Chuxuan -, later known as the "seven perfected", shared a similar social background. All of them had enjoyed a higher education and were skilled in Chinese literature. The first and most important disciple, Ma Danyang, was one of the wealthiest men in the province. Wang's background as a well-educated member of the Chinese elite with a thorough knowledge of literature undoubtedly contributed to his appeal among the elite in Shandong.¹² In addition to recruiting disciples, Wang Chongyang also established five religious societies during the two years he spent in Shandong: In 1186, the *Sanjiao qibao* hui 三教七寶會 ("The society of the three treasures of the three teachings"); in the following year, the *Sanjiao jinlian hui* 三教金蓮會 ("The society of the gold-lotus of the three teachings") in Ninghai; the *Sanjiao sanguang hui* 三教三光會("The society of the three beams of the three teachings") in Fushan; the *Sanjiao yuhua hui* 三教玉華會("The society of the jade-blossoms of the three teachings") in Dengzhou; and the *Sanguang pingdeng hui* 三教平等會("The society of equality of the three teachings") in Laizhou.¹³ After his death his first student Ma Danyang became Wang's successor as the "patriarch" of the new Daoist school. But it was only after the famous Qiu Chuji took over as head of the school that *Quanzhen* gained momentum as a movement among all strata of Chinese society.

---

9 Chin. xiannai 仙耐. See *Lishi zhenxian tidao tongjian xupian*, 1.3a.
10 Ibid.
11 See DZ 296, 1.3b. According to the hagiographical sources, Wang's disciples fulfilled this prophecy when they returned to the village three years later.
12 Florian C. Reiter, "Chung-yang Sets Forth His Teaching In Fifteenth Discourses," in: MS 36 (1984-85), p.36.
13 See T'ao-chung Yao, *Ch'uan-chen: A New Taoist Sect in North China During the Twelfth and Thirteenth Centuries*, Dissertation, University of Arizona, 1980, p.47. and Florian C. Reiter, *Grundelemente und Tendenzen des Religiösen Taoismus*, Wiesbaden 1988, p.65. See also *Qizhen nianpu*, 1.8a -1.8b.

2. Liu Chuxuan's (1147 – 1203) encounter with *Quanzhen*[14]

Rather than providing an exhaustive account of the biography of Liu Chuxuan as it is narrated in the hagiographies, I rely in this section on a non-chronological structure that draws only on examples of the most important narrative elements in the hagiographies. The narratives in the *Quanzhen* hagiographies can be divided into two parts: The life of a master before his enlightenment and his life after enlightenment that led towards immortality. Hence, I will focus first on Liu Chuxuan's awakening to Daoism and the main attributes of his personality before highlighting several incidents that demonstrate his magical powers, moral virtue and relationship with the state and Daoist ritual traditions. From my point of view, the hagiographies should not be read literally. Their main goal resides in reconstructing the lives of the masters as perfect embodiments of the principles of *Quanzhen*.

Liu Chuxuan was 22 years old when he met Wang Chongyang in Shandong. Before he met Wang Chonyang, a mysterious sign[15] appeared on a wall:

---

14 For the discussion of Liu Chuxuan's biography, I rely primarily on his hagiography in the collection of stone inscriptions DZ 973 *Ganshui xianyuan lu* 甘水鮮源錄 and secondarily on DZ 297 *Lishi zhenxian tidao tongjian xupian* 歷世真仙體道通鑒續論. When necessary, I will also add some information found in other hagiographical collections. For a complete translation of Liu Chuxuan's hagiography in DZ 297 *Lishi zhenxian tidao tongjian xupian*, see Florian C. Reiter, *The blending of religious convictions and scholarly notions in the life of the Taoist Patriarch Liu Ch'u-hsüan (1147 –1203)*, in: ZDMG 1997.147.2, p.444-454. The stone inscription found in *Ganshui xianyuan lu* is largely identical to Liu Chuxuan's hagiography in DZ 173 *Jinlian zhengzong ji*. For more bibliographical information on the hagiographic collection see Judith Boltz, *A Survey of Taoist Literature, Tenth to Seventeenth Century*, Berkeley 1987: Berkeley University Press.

15 The appearance of mysterious signs is a common feature of *Quanzhen* hagiographies. Very often, they announce the future enlightenment of the masters or the future appearance of Wang Chongyang. In the hagiography of Ma Danyang, he creates a poem whose meaning he does not understand completely before Wang Chongyang enters his life shortly afterwards: "He traveled to the [estate of] Fan Mingqi to join a banquet at the *Pavilion of the Encounter with an Immortal*. There, he produced a poem whose last sentence read: 'Will there be that man who saves me when I am drunk?' Nobody understood its meaning. The next day, [Wang] Chongyang arrived in Donglai traveling from Zhongnan. He entered the *Pavilion of the Encounter with an Immortal*, and the master [Ma Danyang] asked him: 'Which direction are you coming from?' He replied: 'I came a long way, specifically to help the drunken man.' When the people heard this, everybody was surprised about his words." See DZ 173 *Jinlian zhengzong ji* 3.4b.

> In the spring of the year 1169, he suddenly found two odes written on the wall of the neighboring house, at a place no man could reach. There were still traces of fresh ink, and no author's name was left behind. The last two verses read: "In Wuguan, the soil where the true immortals nurture their inner nature,[16] there must be a man of long life[17] and who does not die." Sighing, the master enjoyed the vigorous strength of the calligraphic stroke, and he wondered about the supernatural transformational potential, yet he could not make up his mind.

Soon enough, his encounter with Wang Chongyang would enlighten the young Liu Chuxan about this mysterious appearance:

> In September of that year, there was cold frost and clear dew, and the founding patriarch Wang Chongyang arrived traveling from the west, accompanied by the three masters of immortality Qiu Chuji, Ma Danyang and Tan Chuduan. Heading towards Haidao, they passed through Shancheng. As soon as the master heard about this, he headed there with great haste and offered incense [to Wang Chongyang]. The founding patriarch looked at him, and he said with a smile: "The signs of ink on the wall – how do you understand them?" The three disciples looked at each other and smiled ironically. They immediately understood the transformation triggered by the spiritual powers of the odes and were shocked by this. The founding patriarch loved [Liu's] diligence, he praised his special essence (*jing* 精) and enjoyed the unusual qualities of his spirit (*shen* 神). Thus, he sighed and said: "The moon of the pine-tree, the snow of the bamboo! Therefore, you are not affected by the yellow dust." Then he dedicated a poem [to Liu]: "He stopped fishing, returned and still saw the *Ao*-turtle. He knows already about the ranks and grades of the immortal officers. Singing in the elm trees, summoning each other: I know your intentions. Go dance on top of the greatest waves, ten thousand zhang high."[18] Thereupon [Liu] grasped the meaning of the words on the wall. Hence, Changsheng 長生 [Long life] became his personal name, Chuxuan 處玄 his Daoist name of honor and Tongmiao 通妙 his style.[19]

The hagiographies in the Daoist Canon describe the young man before his encounter with Wang as a person who followed the basic Confucian rules of conduct, but also as someone who was endowed with extraordinary qualities. Even the circumstances

---

16 Chin. *xing* 性.

17 Chin. *changsheng* 長生. This term is one of the names that Wang Chongyang gave Liu Chuxan after his enlightenment.

18 In DZ 297, 2.6a, we find the same poem. The dedication of a poem is a recurrent motif in the *Quanzhen* hagiographies.

19 It was a common practice in early *Quanzhen* Daoism for the founder Wang Chongyang to choose the new names for his disciples. The wording of DZ 297, 2.6a is clearer: "Thereupon the founding master gave him a personal name and a Daoist name of honor."

of his birth possess a mystical quality.[20] Despite his will to show his filial obedience towards his mother, he feels attracted to the secluded life of a Daoist sage. In other words, the hagiographies introduce him as a young man with conflicting values and aspirations. The death of his father, when Liu was a young boy, forced him to take care of his mother, a demand he fulfilled completely. However, the hagiographies also depict his frequent visits to a famous Daoist spot:

> An orphan from early youth, the master was known for his filial piety towards his mother. [But] he also had the determination for a life in seclusion. Mount Taiji is located about two miles from Wuguan. On the southern ledge of this mountain, there is the valley of the Daoist priest. And this is the place where the prefect of Guangzhou Zheng Daozhao, had attained the Dao. The master often came here for a stroll.[21]

As for his family background, the hagiographies furnish information about the identities of his ancestors, who were known for the respect they paid to moral values. *Ganshui xianyuan lu* provides an extensive account of his family:

> This man from Donglai 東萊 is the perfected man Changsheng, a member of the right [wing] of the *mao-jin* family.[22] The lakes and the seas cannot exhaust his contents, the stars cannot reach up to his high clarity. His ancestors and his parents used to live in Wuguan 武官 for generations. They were great in virtue and happily brought forth mercy; they displayed sympathy for those who live in cold and starvation; they were kind towards those who are orphaned and helpless. They dwelled on fields more than 80 acres in size. And throughout many dynasties, they planted the roots of good fortune. During the period Taiping xingguo 太平興國(976 – 984) the court rewarded the family home for their piety and righteousness.[23] The family was exempted from all services, and they were freed from taxes in the entire commandery Guangzhao 光照.[24]

---

20 See the translation from DZ 297 contained in Florian C. Reiter 1997, pp.444-5. Florian Reiter also points out that a similar story appears in the hagiographies of Wang Chuyi.

21 See DZ 297, 2.5 b. As is the case with other hagiographies of the protagonists of early *Quanzhen* Daoism, the texts do not clearly indicate how Liu Chuxan acquired his basic skills in the performance of Daoist rituals. Nonetheless, we find that most hagiographies mention the actual performance of Daoist rituals by the masters of early *Quanzhen*. Hence, we must assume that Liu and the other disciples received some ritual training before they became followers of Wang Chongyang. However, this is not a topic in this study. For more information on this topic, see Florian C. Reiter 1997, pp. 442-43.

22 *Mao-jin*卯金 is the secret name for the character Liu. It refers to the imperial house of the *Han*-dynasty. See *Zhongwen dacidian*, vol. 2, p. 303.

23 Chin. *xiao*孝and *yi*義, two Confucian virtues.

24 See DZ 973 2.1b.

Like Wang Chongyang himself and the other six famous disciples, Liu stemmed from a wealthy and important family. We can assume that he received a thorough education in classical literature and Confucian philosophy, although the hagiographies devote little attention to a point probably seen as self-evident. However, both *Ganshui xianyuan lu* and *Lishi tidao tongjian xupian* concentrate heavily on the obedience of Liu and his family towards Confucian moral principles. The reader is supposed to learn from the hagiographies that Liu Chuxuan was a man of high virtue even before he encountered Wang Chongyang and experienced his awakening to the truths of *Quanzhen*. In its teachings, *Quanzhen* stresses the importance of morality in its teachings and makes it quite clear that a person of lesser virtue would not qualify for *Quanzhen* self-cultivation.

After his sudden enlightenment through Wang Chongyangs poetry, Liu Chuxuan joined the founder of *Quanzhen* and the other disciples. The group traveled to Wang's ancestral home in Kaifeng and remained with him until his death in the following year 1170.[25] Again, Liu Chuxuan and the other three Qiu Chuji, Ma Danyang and Tan Chuduan followed the Confucian rules of conduct for mourning:

> Together with the other three men, he carried the coffin and returned to mount Zhongnan. They stayed at the mourning shed for three years.[26]

After this period, the group of the four drifted apart. Here, the hagiographies provide a vivid example of the tension between individual approaches towards enlightenment and immortality on the one hand and unifying tendencies on the other. The founder Wang Chongyang had been the great integrative figure in early *Quanzhen* Daoism. After his death, the four most important disciples pursued their individual interests:[27]

> Each of the four disciples had a different will.[28]

---

25 See DZ 175 *Qizhen nianpu* 七真年譜, 8b-9a.
26 See DZ 297, 2.6b.
27 As we will see below, this was not seen as contradictory in early *Quanzhen* Daoism. While every adept practitioner of *Quanzhen* had to obey a set of very general rules, the path towards enlightenment and immortality was a very personal affair.
28 See DZ 973, 3a. Ma Danyang's hagiography contained in DZ 174 *Jinlian zhengyong xianyuan xiangzhuan* 金蓮正宗仙源象傳 has the following story on the different wills of the four masters: "In the year 1174, the master [Ma Danyang] and the three masters Tan, Liu and Qiu lodged at the Shenchenwu temple in Qindu. In a full moon's night, each of them talked about his will. The master [Ma Danyang] said he struggled for poverty. Tan

Hereafter, the hagiographies focus on Liu Chuxuan's spiritual development, elaborately describing several incidents that demonstrate his supernatural powers. After taking leave of the other disciples, Liu spent three years in the temple of the God of the Earth[29] in Kaifeng.[30] Allegedly for the entire time, he failed to utter even a single word. He devoted this period of silence to self-cultivation and the refinement of his asceticism:

> The master stayed by himself in Luojing 洛京 (Kaifeng) cultivating his inner nature amidst the worldly dust and affairs. He nurtured his physical substance in the crowded chaos of the market place and the business districts. The orchestras could not achieve the smoothness of his peace; the flowers and plants could not scratch his essence. When the people offered food to him, he ate; when they did not offer food to him, unlike others he would not become ill-tempered. When the people asked him, he gave them his hand; when they did not ask, he spent the entire day in solitude.[31]

This passage introduces the reader to distinguishing features of Liu Chuxuan's personality. Unlike other practitioners of Daoist self-cultivation, he did not have to retreat from social life.[32] His skills were so honed and his virtue so profound that he could cultivate himself and refine the essentials of his body and mind in an environment wholly alien to such practices.[33] After years of silent self-cultivation, Liu Chuxuan suddenly changed his will:

> When his strength was realized to the fullest and the celestial beams began to shine, he headed to the Clouds Brook Cave. In order to see him, the followers [of Daoism] came across to the grotto. Suddenly he encountered a stone well, containing a source with cold and fresh water. The followers were puzzled about this, and, smilingly, the master said: "There are two more wells here, not much further than several yards. This is the dwelling

---

said he struggled for being. Liu said he struggled for determination. Qiu said he struggled for reclusion."

29 Chin. *tudi miao* 土帝廟.
30 See DZ 297 2.6b.
31 See DZ 973, 2.3a.
32 In his commentary on the *Yinfu jing*, Liu Chuxuan discusses this issue as well. See my translation below. Tan Chuduan's hagiographies record a similar attitude. See Florian C. Reiter, *The Ch'üan-chen Patriarch T'an Ch'u-tuan (1123 – 1185) and the Chinese Talismanic Tradition,* in: ZDMG 146, p.144.
33 The reader may remember the story from the popular novel *Qizhen zhuan* that I quoted in the introduction. In that story, Liu Chuxuan lodges in a brothel without ever giving into any vices. In his commentary on the *Yinfu jing*, this approach towards self-cultivation also becomes an obvious topic. See also the fourth chapter of this study.

ground where I practiced self-cultivation in a former life." And for this reason, this cavern was named Three Sources.³⁴

The hagiographies mention a number of other mysterious incidents. Among these, one occurring in Laizhou in the year 1191 is the most remarkable. While patrolling in Laizhou, a 'commander of the Reserve Horses' noticed that many people had surrounded Liu Chuxuan. Because he could not see anything extraordinary about Liu Chuxuan, the commander became suspicious and had him placed in jail:

> A moment later, the people at the market square saw the master south of the city walls having a conversation with friends of the Dao just like every other day. The prison guard Zheng and the administrator Wang also saw him and suspected that the master had escaped from prison. When they went to the prison to have a look, they found the master there fast asleep. Both of them were very scared, and when they reported everything they had seen the master was released immediately.³⁵

In Liu Chuxuan's commentary on the *Yinfu jing*, we find the expression "the body outside the body."³⁶ Although this expression does not necessarily refer to the ability to appear in different places at the same time, the story above illustrates the application of *Quanzhen* concepts in the hagiographies of the early masters. The expression "the body outside the body" refers to the true persona – both physical and mental – in *Quanzhen* Daoism that is also the eventual outcome of a successful practice of inner alchemy. Here, the hagiography in DZ 297 *Lishi zhenxian tidao tongjian* relies on fantastic elements to elucidate this concept for a wider audience that may have been unfamiliar with the metaphorical language in *Quanzhen* writings.

Even after his enlightenment, Liu Chuxuan did not neglect his filial obligations towards his mother. After the discovery of the three wells, he returned to his birthplace Wuguan to show his respect for her.³⁷ As mentioned above, virtue and moral-

---

34 Ibid. In DZ, 297 2.b, this story is told in a slightly different fashion. See Florian C. Reiter 1997, p.447.
35 See DZ 297, 2.8a. *Ganshui xianyuan lu*, 2.3b, tells a different story: "He did not live there [in Wuguan], and the villagers falsely accused him of murder. Hastily and without a sentence, they tied him up. He spent about 100 days in prison before Chunyang (Lü Dongbin) heard jade leaking. Riding an azure unicorn, he descended from the green clouds and entered the cell. […] He taught him the practice of writing, and then the murderer surrendered himself. Therefore, the master (Liu Chuxuan) escaped from a sentence of imprisonment in chains. When he left, the writing ink [displayed] the greatest mystery and took the shape of dragon and snake flying together."
36 Chin. *shenwai zhi shen* 身外之身.
37 DZ 973, 2.3b.

ity constituted vital parts of *Quanzhen* self-cultivation.³⁸ The practice of healing added yet another significant aspect to the narratives of *Quanzhen* hagiographies. By using their unusual powers in order to heal others, the *Quanzhen* masters fulfilled another requirement of *Quanzhen*.³⁹ An adept practitioner of *Quanzhen* was supposed to live a life beneficial to others, show mercy and compassion and abandon selfish behavior. *Lishi zhenxian tidao tongjian* offers an example of an unusual healing practice. Here, Liu Chuxuan does not use his magical powers to cure a disease. Instead he explains basic *Quanzhen* beliefs to the ill person and teaches him how to live a life in accordance with the Dao:

> The 'bare-footed' Mr. Liu got an illness that after one month was not yet healed. He came to the master to inquire about an early death. Shaking his staff, the master said: "In your lifetime so far, there was a year when you committed the mistake of turning your back to the Dao. In a lifespan, one can use merits to neutralize sins. There are hidden principles according to which both merits and sins receive their retribution.⁴⁰ You can neutralize the sin you committed on a previous day within one year. Since we met each other today, one month will suffice." Thereafter, Mr. Liu swore an oath, and his illness was cured immediately.⁴¹

---

38 The three years of mourning after the death of Wang Chongyang mentioned above were another example for the high moral standards of Liu Chuxuan.

39 For an exhaustive account of healing practices in early *Quanzhen* Daoism, see Stephen Eskildsen, *The Teachings and Practices of the Early Quanzhen Taoist Masters*, New York 2004, p. 57 to 90.

40 In his commentary on the *Yinfu jing*, Liu Chuxuan gives an elaborate explanation of this concept of 'retribution': "The foolish do not know that Heaven will send down calamities and sorrows that befit every mistake they make. They kill and harm pigs and lambs, they burn [paper-]money and [paper-]horses, and they pray. When they are sick, they search for peace. When they encounter calamities, they search for good luck. But they do not know why the non-spirited is a spirit. [My contemporaries] do not know the Dao of the supreme Yang of Heaven. The highest spirits secretly examine every location for the good and the evil in the human realm. When my contemporaries perform good [deeds] three years but no more than a thousand days, [Heaven] sends down auspicious signs and good omens. But when men perform evil [deeds] a thousand days but no more than three years, Heaven sends down calamities and sorrows." See my translation below. In DZ 1141 *Xianle li* 仙樂集, 1.1a-3b, Liu Chuxuan gives a systematic list of evil and good deeds and the compensation of Heaven. See Florian C. Reiter, *The Blending of religious convictions and scholarly notions in the Life of the Taoist Patriarch Liu C'u-hsüan (1147-1203)*, in: ZDMG 147.1997, *fn. 114*.

41 See DZ 297, 2.7b-8a.

The hagiographies contain many other mystical incidents that I will not discuss here. The above quotes provide us with a vivid impression of Liu Chuxuan's personality as it appears in the hagiographies. However, in the context of this study, it is worth mentioning that according to the hagiographies, Liu Chuxuan wrote several commentaries on Daoist classics in the year 1182. Two of these commentaries, one on the *Huangting neijie jing* and the other on the *Yinfu jing*, are still existent in the Daoist Canon. The other commentaries on the *Daode jing* and the *Qingjing jing* have been lost.[42] Liu Chuxuan died in the year 1203 while performing a jiao-ritual. A profound interest in literature distinguished Liu Chuxuan from the other 6 disciples of Wang Chongyang. Except for him, only Hao Datong, whose profession was that of a fortune-teller, produced literary texts other than poetry.[43] The *Recorded Sayings* of Ma Danyang and other disciples were productions of their students. No other disciple of Wang Chongyang wrote a commentary on a classical scripture.

I conclude this section with a quote from *Ganshui xianyuan lu*. Coming at the end of Liu Chuxuan's hagiography, the text mentions an engraving that honors the master:

> The old immortal Changsheng stressed the rules of transformation, he swallowed the void and ejected thusness[44] [from his mouth]. He wandered with the vermillion clouds and traveled below in the corners of the green-blue sea. He joined the congregation at the origin of Heaven, and his destiny was bonded with [Wang] Chongyang for many kalpas. He understood the one hundred passes, he communicated with the nine sources and rode the four beasts. He plowed the three [cinnabar] fields and meditated at the market place of Luoyang. He chiseled a well into the Cloud Brooks Cave, and he mixed the white snow in order to produce a powder. He cooked the dark frost, but it did not evaporate. Talks about his name were spreading in the entire province. His glory illuminated the gold lotus, and

---

42 DZ 973, 2.4b and DZ 174, 33b mention the commentaries on the *Yinfu jing*, but only the *Qingjing jing* and the *Huangting jing*. DZ 297 mentions that Liu Chuxuan wrote other commentaries without specifying them. The *Daoist canon* preserved two other texts attributed to Liu Chuxuan, the poetic anthology DZ 1141 *Xianle ji* and the text DZ 1058 *Wuwei qingjing changsheng zhenren yulu*, which contains Liu's teachings on 81 essential concepts of *Quanzhen* Daoism. Florian C. Reiter assumes that the quotations from the *Daode jing* found in this text stem from Liu's lost commentary on that scripture.

43 See Florian C. Reiter, *The Soothsayer Hao Ta-t'ung (1142-1212) and his Encounter with Ch'üan-chen Taoism*, in: OE 28, 1981.2, p.202. The foreword to DZ 1058 mentions that his teachings attracted many students.

44 Chin. *ziran* 自然.

he erected a residence for the numinous void.[45] He submitted to the order of the court.[46] He returned to Donglai in order to fulfill his family duties. Thereafter, his bones and his flesh dissolved, and he roamed in the eight cardinal celestial heights.[47]

3. The nature of *Quanzhen*, its basic ideas and teachings

The term *Quanzhen* 全真 is a binomial expression. The first word '*quan*' can either be interpreted as a verb, an adverb or a noun. Its literal meaning is 'complete,' 'whole', 'to complete' or 'completion.' The second word '*zhen*' is either a noun or an adverb; its literal meaning is 'truth' or 'true'. In Daoism, it generally refers to a transcendental state of being beyond the comprehension of the average human being. Thus, very often it is also translated as 'perfect' or 'perfection.' In fact, this word is also used for those who have achieved the overarching goal of Daoism: Immortality. The 'perfected man,' *zhenren* 真人, is similar in use to the word 'immortal', *xian* 仙 or *xianren* 仙人. There is also a binomial term comprising of the two words: *zhenxian* 真仙, the 'true' or the 'perfect immortal.' The binomial term *Quanzhen* should be understood as a descriptive expression for a way leading to the goal of perfection: *The completion of perfection*. But due to the peculiarities and grammatical ambiguities of classical Chinese, the term nevertheless also carries the secondary meaning of the goal itself: *The completed perfection*.

Wang Chongyang, the founder of *Quanzhen*-Daoism, never used the term *Quanzhen* in his own writing. However, from the hagiographical sources in the Daoist Canon, we know that he used this term when he encountered Ma Danyang, the first of the famous seven disciples. Ma Danyang had a hut built for Wang Chongyang in his garden. When the hut was finished, Wang Chongyang wrote the two char-

---

45 The gold lotus symbolizes *Quanzhen* here. This name is also part of several religious congregations founded by Wang Chongyang and it appears in the titles of two collections of *Quanzhen* hagiographies.
46 This refers to an incident not included in my discussion of Liu Chuxuan's hagiographies. In 1197, his fame had spread to the capital, and the emperor summoned him to the court and asked about his teachings. See Florian C. Reiter 1997, p.451.
47 Chin. *bajian* 八騫. This term appears in the Daoist encyclopedia DZ 1032 *Yunji qiqian*, 23, 1b. In this text it is linked to the Palace of the Sun: "The Palace of the Sun has the pools of the seven treasures. The eight heights arise from there."

acters for *Quanzhen* on a plate that he then put directly above the entrance to the hut. The message was clear: The master living in this hut was following the ways of complete perfection; those who entered the hut would ultimately submit to this goal.[48]

Although not widely used in Daoist literature before the rise of Wang Chongyang's new school, Wang Chonyang himself did not invent the term *Quanzhen*. It appears in a number of texts that are far more ancient than Wang's writings. The first text that mentions the term is probably the *Zhuangzi*.[49] In chapter 29 of that book, the thief Zhi rejects Confucius' ideas with the following outrage:

> All you [Confucius] have been telling me – I reject everything. Leave immediately now! I do not want to hear any of your talk anymore. Your way [dao] is insane and inadequate. It is fraudulent and clever, an empty and false affair. It cannot [become] complete perfection. How could it be worth discussing?

> 丘之所言,皆吾之所棄也,亟去走歸,復言之!子之道,狂狂汲汲,詐巧虛僞事也,非可以全真也,奚足論哉![50]

The corpus of texts in the Daoist canon attributed to protagonists of early *Quanzhen*-Daoism provides several definitions for the name of the school. The following quote is taken from the text *Jinzhenren yulu* (*Recorded Sayings of the Perfected Man Jin*):

> As for this complete perfection (*Quanzhen*), it is the Dao that accords with the celestial mind. When the spirits do not leave, the *qi* are not dispersed and the essence does not drip; when all these three are kept, the five elements gather and the four signs are in peaceful harmony – this is called 'complete perfection.'

> 夫全真者合天心之道也。神不走、氣不散、精不漏。三者俱備、五行都聚、四象安和、爲之全真也。[51]

---

48 This story appears in DZ 174 *Jinlian zhengzong xianyuan xiangzhuan* 金蓮正宗仙源象傳, 24a and in other hagiographic sources. After a period of one hundred days during which Wang Chongyang taught him about the Dao, Ma Danyang ultimately converted to *Quanzhen* and left his family.

49 The word *Quanzhen* appears in many texts belonging to different currents of religious Daoism. A famous example is the *Miaomen youxi* 妙門由起, a Daoist anthology that was compiled on the order of the Tang-emperor Xuanzong. One of the forewords, dated 713 mentions the term. See DZ *1123 Yiqie jingyi miaomen youqi* 一切經音義妙門由起, *xu*3a.

50 See *Chuang-tsu-yin-te*, Beiping 1948, p. 82.

51 DZ 1056 *Jinzhenren yulu* 晉真人語錄, 8b-9a. For a more comprehensive discussion of the terminology in this text see Florian C. Reiter, *Grundelemente und Tendenzen des re-*

Obviously, this text relates the 'complete perfection' to the basic concepts of *inner alchemy*. The state of being that Wang Chongyang and his seven disciples have in mind is one of perfect harmony. When the three fundamental components of the physical and spiritual being, essence, spirit and *qi*, are stored, balanced and refined, the ideal state of *Quanzhen* or "complete perfection" is attained. This corresponds with inner alchemy's idea that the real immortal could reverse the normal process of life and eventually return to the primordial state of *anterior Heaven*.[52]

In terms of the goal immortality or use of a language and theory related to the context of *inner alchemy*, *Quanzhen* did not differ greatly from many other currents of the Daoist legacy.[53] The most remarkable feature of *Quanzhen* was its eclectic use of content deriving from the *three teachings*.[54] My discussion of Wang Chongyang's life above elucidates that this expression appears in the name of every religious society he established during his two years in Shandong. The "three teachings" referred to here are Daoism, Confucianism and Buddhism, the three 'religions' of classical China.

During the Song- and Jin-dynasties, the idea of harmonizing these three teachings became prevalent.[55] This idea also came to assume a prominent position in the writings of Wang Chongyang and his disciples. Neither Wang nor his disciples invented the idea of harmonization. They merely capitalized on a broader cultural phenomenon, which they integrated into their own religious and philosophical framework.[56] Their texts contain not only quotes or concepts from Daoist classics, but also refer-

---

ligiösen Taoism: Das Spannungsverhältnis von Integration und Individualität in seiner Geschichte zur Chin-, Yüan- und frühen Ming-Zeit, Stuttgart 1988: Franz Steiner, p.73.

52 Liu Changsheng expresses similar thoughts in his commentary on the *Yinfu jing*. For basic principles of *inner alchemy*, see the second chapter of this study.

53 However, due to the diversion into a northern *Jin*-China and a southern *Song*-China, two main Daoist schools of *inner alchemy* were established during this period. The texts attributed to the masters of the Southern school show differences in terminological and conceptual differences from the texts of *Quanzhen*.

54 Chin. *sanjiao*三教. In DZ 1156 *Chongyang zhenren jinguan yusuo jue*重陽真人金關玉鎖訣, 9b Wang Chongyang says: "The three teachings are like the three feet of the tripod." For a more exhaustive analysis of the significance of this key term for the teachings of *Quanzhen*, see Chen Bing, *Lüelun quanzhendao de sanjiao heyi shuo*, in: SJZJYJ, 1.1984, pp. 7-21.

55 See T'ao Chung-yao 1995, p. 97 - 102. T'ao provides an exhaustive account of the history of this term that he traces back to the period of disunity (222 – 589).

56 The idea of a harmonization of the three teachings goes back to early discourses from the third century. See T'ao Ch'ung-yao 1980, p.88.

ences to Confucianism and Buddhism.[57] Yet in spite of its eclectic character, *Quanzhen* remains essentially Daoist in nature, for it preserves the goal of self-cultivation at its core.

Confucianism, in contrast, is focused on the correct ways of governing the country and on general rules of conduct. It aims to produce "gentlemen"[58] who act in accordance with the moral standards established by Confucius and his interpreters. Buddhism believes that the world and its appearances are fundamentally delusional. Its principal goal is to leave the world of suffering behind.[59] A practitioner of *Quanzhen* is determined to become a Daoist immortal. When discussing concepts deriving from Confucianism or Buddhism, the texts of early *Quanzhen* Daoism show a strong tendency towards assimilating the two other teachings to the central goal of Daoism.[60] Wang Chongyang and his disciples do not accept the other teachings as fundamentally different; in their worldview, Buddhism and Confucianism merely appear to be alternate –and sometimes inferior – expressions of the same religious aspirations. In *Chongyang zhenren jinguan yusuo jue*, the three integrative figures of Daoism, Buddhism and Confucianism appear on the same list. Here, Wang Chongyang explains that a person who practices benevolence must rely on the teachings of all three:

> The masters who have not yet learned the practice of self-cultivation, must first grasp [the method] of rescuing and helping others. Those who act [in order to] rescue themselves recline. All those who practice merits and virtue recognize the ancestor, the lineage and the warrant of conduct. The Highest [Lord Lao] is the ancestor. The Buddha is the lineage and Confucius is the warrant of conduct. One follows the three teachings and contemplates in solitude.

---

57 Liu Chuxuan, for example, refers to Confucian virtues in his commentary on the *Yinfu jing* and pays reference to the *Diamond Sutra*, an important Buddhist text. See my translation below.

58 Chin. *junzi* 君子.

59 Hence, Florian C. Reiter argues that the teachings of Buddhism and Daoism were contradictory. See Florian C. Reiter, *Buddhismus und Ch'üan-Chen-Taoismus*, in: MS 42 (1994), p.298.

60 For example, Wang Chongyang and his disciples adopt the term "sudden enlightenment," Chin. *dunwu* 頓悟, from Chan-Buddhism. However, while this term refers to enlightenment to Buddhist truths about the illusionary character of the world, in *Quanzhen* Daoism it designates the consciousness of the perfected man or the Daoist ideal of the immortal. It is worth mentioning that the Chan school itself was deeply influenced by Daoist ideas. See Wing-tsit Chan, *A Source Book in Chinese Philosophy*, Princeton 1973, pp. 425-426.

學修行先持救濟他。人者爲就自己者憑。功德行人各認祖宗科牌。太上爲祖。釋迦爲宗。夫子爲科牌。自從三教既寂已。[61]

The contradictory attitude towards the concept of a 'harmonization of the three teachings' is best shown in a stone inscription entitled *Quanzhen jiaozu pei*:

> As for those three teachings, each of them has its mysterious principles. The Buddhist teachings rely on the mind of the Buddha and the Boddhisatva. In its teachings, this is called *Chan*. Confucianism transmits the school of Confucius and the thought of his disciples. And thus its books call this *the Doctrine of the Mean*. Daoism is derived from the principles of the five thousand words.[62] It is not spoken aloud, yet it is transmitted; it is not acted upon, yet it is achieved. It depends upon the eternal Dao of *non-acting* of the Highest Master Lao. As for the master Wang Chongyang, his teachings call this 'Quanzhen.' It refers to the elimination of errors and delusions and to the sole 'completion' of perfection and to the spirit immortals.

夫三教各有至妙理、釋教得佛之心者、達磨也、其教名之曰禪。儒教傳孔子之家學者、子思也、其書名之曰中庸。道教通五千言之至理、不言而傳、不行而到、居太上老子無爲眞常之道者。重陽子王先生也、其教名之曰全眞。屛去妄幻、獨全其眞者、神仙也。[63]

Clearly, the author was conscious of the fundamental differences between the three teachings. Nonetheless, each of them had its place in *Quanzhen* Daoism under the condition that Buddhist ideas or Confucian concepts would serve the sole Daoist goal of *Quanzhen*: Immortality.

Quanzhen self-cultivation does not focus on the mind or the body; nor is its brand of self-cultivation primarily an inner activity. In the worldview of *Quanzhen*, those who want to become an immortal or a *perfected man* must follow a twofold process. First, this process needs to comprise an outer practice of asceticism and a living based on virtue and moral principles often derived from the Confucian legacy. At the same time, it entails an inner practice that relies on the principles of *inner alchemy* that I elaborated in the first chapter of this study.

The texts of early *Quanzhen* often discuss the theme of a "double cultivation of inner nature and existence,"[64] which according to Daoist philosophy together consti-

---

61 DZ 1156,14b.
62 Here, the text refers to the *Daode jing*, which is also known as the "scripture of the five thousand words."
63 *Quanzhen jiaozu pei,* in: *Ganshui xianyuan lu*, 1.2b. For a modern edition of the text, see Chen Yuan (ed.), *Daojia jinshilüe*, p.450-454.
64 Chin. *xingming shuangxiu*性命雙修.

tute the complete human being. While "inner nature" refers to the spiritual aspects of a human being, the term "existence" applies to his physical life. *Quanzhen* represents a new approach to the topic of immortality because it insists that this goal cannot be attained if one neglects either inner nature or existence. Hence, the discourse on self-cultivation and *inner alchemy* as it appears in the writings of Wang Chongyang and his disciples assumes a markedly different outlook from other contemporary or more ancient Daoist schools. In the text *Chongyang lijiao shiwulun* for example, Wang Chongyang stresses the importance of a dual cultivation of inner nature and existence in the following words:

> Being (*hsing* 性) – this is the spiritual agent. Existence (*ming* 命) – this is the vital energy. If *hsing* meets with *ming*, this resembles a bird which, feeling the wind, rises gracefully and easily.[65]

In *Chongyang shou danyang ershisi jue*, Wang Chongyang explains the two terms by using terminology derived from *inner alchemy*:

> Danyang also asked: 'What is called seeing being and existence?' The master [Wang Chongyang] replied: 'Being, this is the original spirit. Existence, this is the original *qi*. And the name [for both of them] is being and existence'. Ma Danyang inquired further: 'What is called the roots and the stems?' The master replied: 'The roots, this is being. Existence, this is the stems.'

> 丹陽又問：何名見性命。祖師答曰：性者是元神，命者是元氣，名曰性命。丹陽又問：何名爲根蔕。祖師答曰：根者是性，命者是蔕[66]

This metaphor indicates that being and existence are seen as intrinsically one. They complement each other just like the roots and stems of a plant. Without the roots, the plant would not come into being; without the stems it would not grow leaves or flowers.

The practitioner of *Quanzhen* does not have to follow the fundamental principle of self-cultivation alone. Compliance with strict rules of asceticism and a life based on moral principles possesses a significance equal to the "dual cultivation of inner nature and existence". Along these lines, the adept practitioner of *Quanzhen* must refrain from vices. The following quote is taken from *Wang Chongyang zhenren jinguan yusuo jie*:

---

65 DZ 1233. The translation follows Florian C. Reiter, "*Ch'ung-Yang sets forth his Teachings in Fifteen Discourses,*" *A Concise Introduction to the Taoist Way of Life of Wang Che*, in: MS 36 (1984-85), p. 51. This section also features a quote from the *Yinfu jing*.

66 DZ 1157 *Chongyang shou danyang ershisi jue* 重陽授丹陽二十四訣, 1a.

And he [Wang Chongyang] was asked what the mysterious principles of the cultivation of perfection were. He answered: "The first [principle] is to abandon the nameless vexations. The second [principle] is to give up desires, affectionate love, wine, sensuality, wealth and anger. These are simply the laws of cultivation and practice."

或問曰：如何是修真妙理。答曰：第一，先除無名煩惱。弟二，休愛酒色氣。此者便是修行之法。[67]

Similar lists of vices crop up quite frequently in Wang Chongyang's writings, as well as in the writings of his seven disciples. As illustrated in my discussion of Liu Chuxan's hagiographies, only a person who refrains from all vices qualifies for *Quanzhen* self-cultivation.

However, refraining from vices alone is not sufficient. In order to fulfill the requirements of early *Quanzhen* Daoism, an adept was supposed to leave his family and retreat from the society of worldly men.[68] Many of the hagiographies in the Daoist Canon that chronicle the lives of Wang Chongyang's seven disciples devote significant attention to Wang Chongyang's attempts at convincing them to leave their families and loosen their social ties. Only in doing so would the followers of *Quanzhen* be able to free themselves from mundane emotions, desires and preoccupations that would otherwise remain obstacles on the path towards immortality and perfection.[69]

With its demand for a complete retreat from a mundane life, *Quanzhen* marks the greatest departure from the ways of *Zhengyi* Daoism. Before the appearance of *Quanzhen*, Daoism did not know any schools that were primarily focused on a monastic life. However, in the early days of *Quanzhen*, the demand for a secluded life did not lead to the establishment of monasteries. This was a much later development. As for the *seven perfected*, the rules imposed by Wang Chongyang did not yield a completely homogeneous approach towards the common goal of immortality. Each of them established his personal tradition and lineage. While the sources in the Daoist canon illustrate that the seven disciples shared many basic concepts and ideas, their texts also reveal differences that are mirrored in the hagiographies I explored in the last section. Nevertheless, most of these differences are comparatively minor

---

67 DZ 1156,1a.
68 Chin. *shiren*世人. This term occurs frequently in Liu Chuxuan's commentary.
69 See DZ 1233,1a. In the first discourse, Wang Chongyang argues about those who "leave their families" (Chin. *chujia*出家): "Everyone who leaves his family (ch'u-chia出家) has first to surrender himself to a retreat (*an*庵). A retreat is a shelter, a resort for one's whole life. If the physical existence (*shen*身) does have such a resort, then the mind (*hsin*心) will gradually achieve quietness." See Florian C. Reiter 1984, p.41.

in nature. The final chapter of the study will explore which elements of Liu Chuxuan's theory incorporate the general concepts of early *Quanzhen* Daoism and compare these with those that reflect the unique features of his own personality.

3

The *Huangdi Yinfu Jing* and its Significance in *Quanzhen* Daoism

This chapter is divided into two sections. The first section deals with the *Yinfu jing* itself. I discuss the unknown origins of the scripture and the basic concepts described within it. In the second section, I first address the general significance of reading and classics in *Quanzhen* Daoism before moving on to elucidate the special role of the *Yinfu jing* and purpose of Liu Chuxuan's commentary on it. My analysis here is intended to show how the broader currents of Chinese intellectual history and basic persuasions of *Quanzhen* Daoism influenced Liu Chuxuan's text.

1. Authorship, date and basic content of the scripture

The *Huangdi yinfu jing* 黃帝陰符經 (*The Yellow Emperor's Scripture of the Hidden Contracts*), also known under the shorter title *Yinfu jing* 陰符經, is one of the most sacred texts in religious Daoism. The *Zhengtong Daozang*, the Daoist Canon, contains about 30 commentaries on the scripture, most of which were written in the Song- and the Yuan-dynasty.[1] Along with the *Zhuangzi* 莊子, the *Daode jing* 道德經 and the *Zhouyi cantong qi* 周易參同契, it ranks as one of the most frequently com-

---

1 Florian C. Reiter, *The "Scripture of the Hidden Contracts" (Yin-fu ching), a Short Survey on Facts and Findings*, in: NOAG 1984, 136, p.75.

mented on classical Daoist texts.² It is also known as one of the 'Five Daoist Classics and Four Daoist Books.'³ However, the *Yinfu jing* did not arouse the interest of Daoist writers alone; numerous commentaries exist outside the Daoist canon authored not by Daoists but Confucianists and other scholars.⁴ The *Yinfu jing kaoyi* 陰符經考意, written by the famous neo-Confucian philosopher Zhu Xi, represents the most noteworthy example of such a non-Daoist commentary on the *Yinfu jing*.⁵

The precise origins of the *Yinfu jing* are shrouded in mystery. Many sources associate the scripture with Li Quan 李筌, the author of the first known commentary on the text, and the Daoist Kou Qianzhi 寇謙之 (386-534), who initiated the reform movement of *Zhengyi*-Daoism during the Northern Wei-dynasty. Du Guanting's 杜光庭 (850-933) *Tales of Encounters with Spirit Immortals* (*Shenxian ganyu zhuan* 神仙感遇傳) contains the following account of Li Quan's discovery of the *Yinfu jing*:

> Li Quan, styled Da Guanzi, lived in the Shaoshi Mountains and was fond of the Dao of the immortals. He traveled frequently to famous mountains in search of recipes and Daoist techniques. When he arrived at the Tiger Mouth Rock of Mount Song, he discovered *The Yellow Emperor's Hidden Contracts*. It was written on white silk cloths with red lacquer marks serving as chapter headings. The heading on the jade case containing the text says: 'On the seventh day of the seventh month of the first year of the *zhenjun*-period of the Great Wei, the Highest Clarity Daoist Kou Qianzhi buried this book in this mountain. He hoped that it would be transmitted to an equally worthy person.' Although the book was

---

2   Judith Boltz, *A Survey of Taoist Literature, Tenth to Seventeenth Century*, Berkeley 1987: University of California, p.203.
3   Chin *daojiao wujing* sishu 道教五經四書. The other four classics are the *Dadejing* 道德經, the *Qingjing jing* 清精經 and the *Longhu jing* 籠虎經. The 'four books' are the *Cantong qi* 參同契, the *Wuzhen pian* 悟真篇, the *Sanhuang yujue* 三皇玉訣 and the *Qinghua miwen* 青華秘文. See *Daojiao dacidian*, p.945.
4   According to Gong Pengcheng, more than a thousand scholars have produced commentaries on the *Yinfu jing*. See Gong Pengcheng, *Daojiao xinlun*, Taibei 1990: Taiwan Xuesheng, p.299.
5   See Florian C. Reiter 1984, p.76. For a discussion of Zhu Xi's commentary see Julia Ching, *Chu His and Taoism*, in: Irene Bloom and Joshua A. Fogel (eds.), *Meeting of Mind*, New York 1996: Columbia University Press, pp. 127-123. It is noteworthy that the *Yinfu jing* is the first book mentioned in the section on Daoist literature in the imperial catalogue *Siku quanshu zongmu*. This catalogue lists the *Yinfu jing* and three commentaries on the scripture. The first commentary listed is the one authored by Zhu Xi. See *Siku quanshu zongmu*, Beijing 1965, vol. 2, p.1241-2.

decrepit, Li Quan copied it. He read it a thousand times, yet he was not able to grasp its meaning and its principles.[6]

Du Guanting's claim that Li Quan was unable to comprehend the meaning of the *Yinfu jing* is important for two reasons. On the one hand, Li Quan's commentary represents one of the most famous and significant references for other texts in religious Daoism. On the other, some scholars, including the aforementioned Zhu Xi, have suggested that Li Quan wrote the *Yinfu jing* himself.

Modern Chinese scholars have attacked this claim. According to these scholars, Li Quan's commentary and the *Yinfu jing* contrast too starkly in their literary style. It has also been suggested that Kou Qianzhi was the author of the *Yinfu jing*. However, the metaphysical content of the *Yinfu jing* differs greatly from Kou Qianzhi's primary interests in Daoist liturgy, morality and his political ambitions.[7] Ultimately then, the authorship and origin of the scripture remain as ambiguous as they were in ancient times.[8]

One of the scripture's central concepts provides a clue to the earliest possible date of its inception. In the *Yinfu jing*, Heaven is associated with the 'five bandits':

> To perceive the Way of Heaven and grasp the phases of Heaven is to exhaust all. Thus Heaven has five bandits and he who detects them will be brilliant.[9]

The concept of thievery and the representation of the five elements as 'bandits' made its first appearance in the *Book Liezi*, a Daoist scripture believed to stem from the times of the eastern Jin dynasty.[10] Since there is no record of the scripture dating

---

6 DZ 298 *Shenxian ganyu zhuan*神仙感遇傳, 1.11a.
7 See David C. Yu, (transl.), *History of Chinese Daoism; Vol. 1*, London, New York, Oxford 2000: University Press of America, p. 368. For a concise account of Kou Qianzhi and his activities under the rule of the northern Wei, please consult Richard B. Mather, *K'ou Ch'ien-chih and the Taoist Theocracy at the Northern Wei Court, 425–451*, in: Holmes Welch and Anna Seidel (eds.), *Facets of Taoism*, New Haven and London 1979: Yale University Press, p.103-122.
8 See Florian C. Reiter 1984, p.76.
9 See my translation of Liu Chuxuan's commentary below.
10 In the *Book Liezi*, a Mr. Guo explains: "I have heard it said: 'Heaven has its seasons, earth has its benefits.' I rob heaven and earth of their seasonal benefits, the clouds and rain of their irrigating floods, the mountains and marshes of their products, in order to grow my crops, plant my seed, raise my walls, build my house. I steal birds and animals from the land, fish and turtles from the water. All this is stealing." See A. C. Graham, *The Book of Lieh-tzu*, London 1960: John Murray, pp. 30-31.

from earlier periods of Chinese history, I follow David C. Yu's conclusion that the author of the *Yinfu jing* must have known the *Book Liezi* and used it as a source.[11]

The *Yinfu jing* is a very short text. There are numerous editions of the scripture, many of which exist outside the Daoist Canon.[12] The scripture also circulates in two different versions, one of which is considerably longer than the other. While the version used by Li Quan, Liu Chuxuan and most other Daoist commentators contains about three hundred characters, the other version has over four hundred.[13] Except for the added characters at the end however, the longer version is almost identical with the shorter one.[14]

Most known editions of the *Yinfu jing* employ headings to divide the text into three parts:

The upper chapter: The spirit immortal embraces the One: On the Dao.

The middle chapter: Enriching the state and pacifying the people: On law.

The lower chapter: Strengthening soldiers for victories in battles: On [military] methods.

Allegedly, Li Quan added these headings to the scripture. According to the legend narrated in the *Shenxian ganyu zhuan*, Li Quan could not make any sense of the scripture until he encountered an old, immortal woman who explained the text to him by using the exact headings found in most existent editions of the text:

And thus she sat down explaining the meaning of the *Hidden Contracts* to Li Quan. She said: 'This *Contract* contains three hundred words. One hundred words are on the Dao. One hundred words are on the law. One hundred words are on the arts [of war]. The upper chapter is on how the spirit immortals embrace the One. The middle chapter is on enriching the state and pacifying the people. The lower chapter is on strengthening soldiers for victory in battle.[15]

Despite its extreme brevity, the *Yinfu jing* is a very complex and esoteric work. The remarkable number of commentaries on the scripture, both within the Daoist canon

---

11 David C. Yu goes a step further and suggests a probable date between 531 and 580 as the origin of the *Yinfu jing*. See David C. Yu, 2000, p.367. Isabel Robinet supports this position. See Robinet, *Taoism: Growth of a Religion*, Stanford 1997: Stanford University Press, p.210.
12 Many editions are listed in Christopher C. Rand, 1979, p.133, fn. 47.
13 The shorter *Yinfu jing* is also the basis for DZ 31 *Yinfu jing*. The longer version does not exist as an independent scripture in the Daoist Canon.
14 Christopher C. Rand thinks that the shorter version is also the older text.
15 DZ 298 *Shenxian ganyu zhuan*, 12a.

and elsewhere, also derives from the almost impenetrable nature of the concepts it contains. In short, the *Yinfu jing* creates a space for variegated interpretations. Li Quan, as well as many other commentators, understood the *Yinfu jing* as a treatise on the strategies of war. However, I want to follow Liu Chuxuan's commentary here and redirect the focus towards the metaphysical concepts that structure the text.

Many of the concepts delineated in the *Yinfu jing* are essentially Daoist in nature. The relationship between the 'three cosmic substances'[16] of the Chinese and Daoist intellectual heritage forms the core of the *Yinfu jing*. These 'substances' are Heaven, Man and Earth, and their order is not accidental. Man stands between Heaven and Earth, and his relations with both determine his existence. Hence, understanding these relations helps Man lead a profitable and suitable life. Heaven, on the other hand, refers not only to the physical space above, but also the realm of the divine. And finally, Earth represents quite literally the soil on which man stands, but at the same time, more metaphorically, the adversary to the celestial forces of Chinese cosmology.

In the *Yinfu jing*, the interdependency of the three cosmic forces Heaven, man and Earth is symbolized in the concept of thievery. According to the *Yinfu jing*, Heaven is constituted by the presence of *five bandits*. Like many other commentators, Liu Chuxuan identifies these *five bandits* with the five elements or agents of Chinese cosmology.[17] Thus, the thievery triggered by Heaven and its bandits is nothing more than the cosmological principle of creation.[18] Thievery is essentially a mutually determining process that unifies Heaven, man and Earth. Quite obviously, this aspect of the *Yinfu jing* captured the attention of the *inner alchemy* authors. The theory of the five elements is, as discussed in the first chapter of this study, one of the constitutive elements of *inner alchemy*.

The metaphor of the 'five bandits' is based on the characteristic Daoist idea of correspondence between macrocosmic and microcosmic processes,[19] and as in *inner alchemy*, the *Yinfu jing* suggests that a saint can reverse the normal cause of nature if he proves capable of adapting to the Dao of Heaven. The similarities between the structure of the *Yinfu jing* and the theory of *inner alchemy* are striking. Hence, it is

---

16 Chin. *sancai*三才.
17 For a short discussion of the theory of the five elements see the second chapter of this study.
18 See Zhang Jiyu and Li Yuanguo, "*Mutual Stealing among the Three Powers*" in the *Scripture of Unconscious Unification*, in N.J. Girardot, James Miller and Liu Xiaogan (eds.), Cambridge 2001: Cambridge University Press, p.114.
19 See Florian C. Reiter 1994, p.77.

unsurprising that it became one of the most frequently commented on Daoist scriptures and an indispensable source for all schools of *inner alchemy*.

2. The role of the classics and the significance of the *Yinfu jing* in early *Quanzhen* Daoism

As discussed in the second chapter of this study, Wang Chongyang, Liu Chuxuan and Wang's other disciples all came from wealthy families and received a thorough training in classical Chinese literature. The Daoist Canon provides testimony of their literary ambitions in a sizeable collection of poetry ascribed to them.[20] With the lone exception of Sun Bu'er, each of them is represented with at least one collection. Beyond the poetry collections, the Daoist Canon furnishes an impressive array of texts on different topics that were written by proponents of early *Quanzhen* Daoism. In other words, literature and writing constituted an unambiguously important aspect of their lives.

Especially in texts dealing with matters of self-cultivation, it becomes quite obvious that all masters of early *Quanzhen* Daoism drew heavily on an extensive knowledge of classical scriptures. However, the scriptures mentioned or quoted in those texts do not necessarily belong to the traditional Daoist heritage. Many quotations derive from the *Yinfu jing*, but others trace their origins to Confucian or Buddhist scriptures. Apparently, the notion of a harmonization between the 'three teachings' was more than a slogan. It was common practice to refer to Buddhist scriptures such as the *Xin jing* 心經 (*Heart Sutra*) and the *Jingang jing* 金剛經 (*Diamond Sutra*),[21] as well as to the Confucian classic *Xiao jing* 孝經 (*Classic of Filial Piety*). However, the most frequently quoted texts are the *Daode jing* and the *Yinfu jing*.

Today, it is difficult to determine what role the study of classical scriptures played in early *Quanzhen* Daoism. From the existing sources in the Daoist Canon,

---

20 For a complete list and short discussion of the available collections see Tao-chung Yao, *Quanzhen – Complete Perfection*, in: Livia Kohn (ed.), *Daoist Handbook*, pp. 573-576. A discussion of the literary form and content of several poems composed by masters of early *Quanzhen* can be found in Huang Taohan, *Quanzhen qizi ci shuping*, in: *Xianggang wenhua yanjiousuo xuebao* 19, 1988, pp. 135-162.
21 In his commentary, Liu Chuxuan mentions the *Diamond Sutra* and relates its concept of the "four perceptions" to central ideas contained in the *Yinfu jing*.

the reader gains an almost contradictory picture. And indeed, early *Quanzhen* Daoism shows a highly ambivalent attitude towards the study of classical scriptures. On the one hand, the masters of early *Quanzhen* Daoism frequently mention and quote classical scriptures, several of which were understood to provide fundamental access to the essentials of self-cultivation. On the other, it becomes quite clear from their writings that reading literature could never be a stand-alone method for the attainment of immortality. Classical literature plays a supporting role along a more arduous road towards sainthood.

The text *Chongyang lijiao shiwulun* 重陽立教十五論 (*Chongyang sets forth his teachings in fifteen discourses*) epitomizes this ambivalence perfectly:

> The real method of studying books is not to strive after literary accomplishments (*wen* 文) and thereby to confuse one's eyes. One should properly grasp the meaning (of the books) and have it accord with one's own mind (*hsin* 心). So one puts the books aside, researches their meaning and grasps the principles, (Then) one sets the principles aside and grasps one's (own) thoughts (*ch'ü* 趣). Having a hold on one's own (thoughts, one can store them within the mind). (Practicing this) a very long time in sincerity, naturally the spiritual radiance of the mind (*hsin-kuang* 心光) will then be overflowingly rich.[22]

According to Wang Chongyang, the scholarly methods of China's traditional class of literati are worthless in the pursuit of immortality. If one studies the classical scriptures without relating them to a personal practice, the studies remain a vain and useless occupation. A scholar who dissects a text without practicing the methods it provides cannot understand its true meaning.[23]

Hence, a commentary such as Liu Chuxuan's on the *Yinfu jing* performs the role of a didactic book and could only function as a mere introduction to secret practices. It gives access to the text for the initiated practitioner so that he can use it in self-cultivation. The language, however, had to be coded, and not only to prevent the uninitiated from gaining access to a secret wisdom. The quote above relates the meaning of a text to the thoughts of the individual. A commentary can only serve as an

---

22 DZ 1233. The quote is taken from Florian C. Reiter, "*Ch'ung-Yang sets forth his Teachings in fifteen Discourses*": *A Concise Introduction to the Taoist Way of Wang Che*, in: MS 36 (1984-85), pp.44-45.

23 In DZ 1057 *Danyang zhenren yulu* 丹陽真人語錄, 10a, Ma Danyang goes further by claiming that studying scriptures can disturb the mind of a student. In the same passage he recommends two texts, each with one commentary for occasional reading: The *Daode jing* with the *Heshang gong* commentary and the *Yinfu jing* with a commentary written by the Daoist Jin Lingzi or Tang Chun, DZ 121 *Huangdi yinfu jing zhu*.

introduction, not as a complete explanation. Only the practitioner himself would be able to grasp the meaning of the classics in its entirety.

What was the significance of the *Yinfu jing* in early *Quanzhen* Daoism? A hagiography dealing with the life of Wang Chongyang mentions both the *Daode jing* and the *Yinfu jing* as the scriptures that were essential for his teachings.[24] The fact that both scriptures appear in this context illuminates the crucial role of the *Yinfu jing*. The *Daode jing* is the most sacred scripture not only in *Quanzhen*, but also in other schools. For the proponents of early *Quanzhen* Daoism, the *Yinfu jing* enjoyed an equally high esteem with that text. In the words of Wang Chongyang:

> In order to attain immortality, one must fully understand the three hundred characters of the *Yinfu jing* and read the five thousand words of the *Daode jing*.

理透陰符三百字搜通道德五千言。[25]

In the first chapter of this study, I drew on the text *Dadan zhizhi*, which is ascribed to Qiu Chuji. The text makes extensive use of quotes derived from the *Yinfu jing* and refers to the scripture as the *Classic of the Immortals* (*xian jing* 仙經).[26] Attaining immortality comprised the most important goal for early *Quanzhen*, as it remains today. In *Chongyang jinguan yusuo jue*, Wang Chongyang devotes significant attention to expounding the topics derived from the *Yinfu jing*.[27] And Liu Chuxuan did not only write a commentary on the *Yinfu jing*. In the text *Wuwei qingjing changsheng zhenren yulu* 無爲清靜長生真人語錄, he also drew heavily on the scripture.

Why did the *Yinfu jing* play such a great role in the writings of Wang Chongyang and his disciples? In the last section, I briefly discussed the most fundamental concepts appearing in the *Yinfu jing* and explained why those concepts attracted the interest of the Daoist masters occupied with *inner alchemy*. The foreword to Liu

---

24 See DZ 173 *Jinlian zhengzong ji* 金蓮正宗記, 2.2a.
25 DZ 1153 *Chongyang quanzhen ji* 重陽全真集13.7b.
26 See DZ 244 *xu, 1a*. The foreword to Liu Chuxuan's commentary uses this term as well. See DZ 122, *xu*, 1b.
27 In this text, the *Yinfu jing* is ascribed to Laozi: "Laojun [Laozi] wrote down the subtle sayings of the three vehicles. Each practice reduces the sins and each sentence extends life (*changsheng*長生). The upper chapter has: 'The Spirit Immortal embraces the One.' The middle chapter has: 'Enriching the state and pacifying the people: On law.' The lower chapter has: 'Strengthening soldiers for victories in battles: On [military] methods.' Following this introduction, the reader finds an in-depth discussion of each chapter heading. See DZ 1156, 4a.

Chuxuan's commentary sheds light on the fundamental notions contained in the *Yinfu jing* according to the teachings of *Quanzhen*:

> As for the more than three hundred characters of the *True Scripture of the Hidden Contracts*, its language is simple but the meaning is detailed, its style is deep but the affairs [covered] are complete. Heaven and Earth's trigger of life and death, the principles of the creational process of Yin and Yang, the true outcome of the subtle applications – all this is contained and exhaustively covered in it.[28]

This foreword is quite straightforward in its appraisal of the *Yinfu jing*. The author does not merely believe that the text provides essential ideas or concepts for the practitioner of *Quanzhen*. Despite the brevity and linguistic simplicity of the *Yinfu jing*, he is convinced that the ideas expressed in it cover the entire 'affairs' of the Daoist cosmos. In the first chapter of this study, I explained that *inner alchemy* was based on the assumption that a fundamental knowledge of cosmological principles would eventually lead the practitioner of *Quanzhen* and other schools to immortality. The above quote indicates that a thorough study of the *Yinfu jing* would suffice to provide this knowledge.

---

28 DZ 122, *xu*, 1a.

4

Liu Chuxuan's Commentary and his Theory of Self-Cultivation

1. Introduction

The central topic of this study is Liu Chuxuan's theory of self-cultivation contained in his commentary on the *Yinfu jing*. In the first chapter, I explained some of the fundamental concepts of *inner alchemy* that informed Liu Chuxuan's theory. The second chapter dealt with the *Quanzhen* school with which Liu Chuxuan was affiliated. In the following chapter, I delineated the reasons why the *Yinfu jing* serves as one of the most important sources of reference for the masters of early *Quanzhen* Daoism. This final and concluding chapter discusses the Daoist project of self-cultivation at the level of Liu Chuxuan's texts.

Throughout this study, I have argued that Liu Chuxuan's commentary functions as a didactic instruction. It explains the secret meanings of the *Yinfu jing* that are hidden in its coded and esoteric language, making them available for the practitioner's self-cultivation. The foreword to Liu Chuxuan's commentary supports this interpretation:

> The perfected man and father Liu Changsheng of the spirit's mountains teaches the methods and provides the implementations. He is a master and teacher with extraordinary talents. He studied antiquity and presence thoroughly. His mind roams in the realm of Dao and De.[1] And pondering deeply, he examined the essentials, he obtained the mysteries and

---

1 *Dao* and *De*, "the way" and "virtue" are the two central concepts and themes in the *Daode jing*.

uncovered the hidden secrets [of the *Yinfu jing*] and produced comments and explanations [of this]. Clearly, his comprehension of change and his knowledge of the practice of change[2] benefits those men who follow him. That can be called compassion and mercy. This is the application of a benevolent man's mind. At Ji'nan he guarded perfection and ordered me to produce this foreword. He wishes it to circulate widely and everywhere, may it serve as a compass for the students, so that they can scrutinize the elegant style in detail. By using [this text] they will awake from their doubts and lies, and all of them will leave the net of dust.[3]

The author of this foreword has a very specific understanding of the purpose of Liu Chuxuan's writing. He does not attribute its primary value to its literary qualities, but rather characterizes Liu Chuxuan as a "teacher with extraordinary talents." In revealing the "hidden secrets" of a scripture as central as the *Yinfu jing*, Liu Chuxuan's commentary leads students to a correct practice of self-cultivation. Any reader who studies Liu Chuxuan's commentary thoroughly will ultimately achieve the enlightenment that a practitioner of *Quanzhen* Daoism seeks.

Instead of taking a purely scholarly approach to a sacred scripture in his commentary,[4] Liu Chuxuan attempts to explicate the theory of self-cultivation that the masters of early *Quanzhen* believed was contained in the *Yinfu jing*. In doing so, the commentary applies core *Quanzhen* beliefs to the scripture. However, the text is much more complex than it may seem at a first glance. The masters of early *Quanzhen* Daoism strongly believed *Quanzhen* was nothing more than the correct interpretation of the concepts in both the *Daodejing* and the *Yinfu jing*. From their point of view, the teachings of *Quanzhen* were an explication of these two texts, not

---

2 I.e. a core element of the theory of *inner alchemy* derived from the *Yijing* and the *Zhouyi cantongqi*.

3 DZ 122, *xu* 1a-b. The author of this foreword was a man named Fan Yi. He was the author of the forewords to a number of texts ascribed to Wang Chongyang and his disciples, among them DZ 1153 *Chongyang quanzhen ji*, DZ 1154 *Chongyang jiaohu ji* and DZ 1160 *Shuiyun ji*. His foreword to Liu Chuxuan's commentary is dated 1191. Assuming the accuracy of this date, Liu Chuxuan must have written his commentary between 1182 and 1191. The first date is derived from Liu Chuxuan's hagiography in DZ 297. Fan Yi appears as the author of the forewords of DZ 1153 *Chongyang quanzhen ji*, DZ 1154 *Chongyang jiaohu ji* and DZ 1160 *Shuiyun ji*.

4 This argument does not imply that Liu Chuxuan's commentary shows no traits of a scholarly approach. However, in this study I do not focus on these issues. Florian C. Reiter discusses the topic of Liu Chuxuan's "scholarly notions," noting several sources that include his commentary on the *Yinfu jing*. See Florian C. Reiter, 1997, passim.

merely one interpretation among others.⁵ Hence, when commenting on the *Yinfu jing*, Liu Chuxuan probably believed that he was not adding anything to the scripture, but rather coaxing out meanings already embedded within its coded language.

Liu Chuxuan's commentary dissects the text of the *Yinfu jing* into parts, sometimes explaining whole sentences, sometimes exploring separate words. It belongs to the literary genre of the *zhangju*-commentaries. Literally, the term *zhangju* translates as "section and sentence" and hails from a long tradition in China. The *Heshang gong* commentary on the *Daodejing*, also cited in Liu Chuxuan's text, represents one of the most noteworthy examples of this style.⁶

In the ensuing sections of this chapter, I do not provide an exhaustive account of Liu Chuxuan's commentary. Instead, I focus on two critical themes that structure the text. First, Liu Chuxuan follows the tradition of dividing the *Yinfu jing* into three chapters with the respective headings that I outlined in the third chapter of this study. This division provides the foundation for his interpretation of the scripture as a description of self-cultivation in three successive stages. The second central theme I explore is the description of the Dao of Heaven and related distinction between "worldly men" and "sages." In the next section, I will discuss this latter theme, focusing on the "Dao of Heaven" and the fundamental cosmological notions related to it. I then move on to explore Liu Chuxuan's threefold theory of self-cultivation.

2. The Dao of Heaven and cosmological notions

At the core of Liu Chuxuan's theory of self-cultivation the reader encounters the term "Dao of Heaven."⁷ It represents the totality of celestial principles that shape and inform "the creational process"⁸ and the ten thousand beings. The "Dao of

---

5 See the quote taken from Wang Chongyang's anthology in my last chapter.
6 See Alan K. L. Chan, *A Tale of Two Commentaries: Ho-Shang-Kong and Wang-Pi on the Lao-Tzu*, in: Livia Kohn and Michael LaFargue (eds.), *Lao-tzu and the Tao-te-ching*, New York 1998, pp. 90–91.
7 This term hails from a long tradition. In the *Daode jing*, it is used as the opposite to the "Dao of man" (Chin. *rendao* 人道). The Daode jing associates the "Dao of Heaven" with the central term "non-acting" (Chin. *wuwei* 無爲). Hence, the term "Dao of Heaven" implies a secondary meaning. It not only designates the celestial principles, but also the rules of conduct that the sages follow.
8 Chin. *zaohua* 造化.

Heaven" pervades the entire cosmos and is present even in the minutest particles.[9] Hence, no being could escape its rule, and yet, the "Dao of Heaven" remains hidden and impenetrable to the normal human mind and consciousness. While its applications are visible and its outcomes affect every human being, it operates secretly under the surface of physical reality. When describing the Dao, Liu Chuxuan repeatedly illuminates its paradoxical character. In DZ 1058, for example, he makes this quite obvious:

> As for the Dao, it penetrates matter. If matter is absent, there is Dao. If one knows emptiness and the absence of emptiness, then there are the eternal rules. And this is called "the eternal rules of the Dao."

> 道者通物。無物則道也。知空而不空則常也。謂之道常也。[10]

Liu Chuxuan's notions echo those contained in the first chapter of the *Daode jing*. He uses the fundamental Daoist terminology derived from this sacred text:

> The Dao that is [known as] the Dao is not the eternal Dao / The name that is [known as] the name is not the eternal name / Non-being, this is the name of the origin of Heaven and Earth / Being, this is the name of the mother of the ten thousand beings.

> 道可道，非常道；名可名，非常名。無，名天地之始；有，名萬物之母。[11]

Under the cosmological conditions of later Heaven, the Dao causes the energetic exchanges of *Yin* and *Yang*. In his descriptions of those exchanges, Liu Chuxuan relies on cosmological speculations hailing from a long tradition in religious Daoism[12] in

---

9 See DZ 122.10b. Commenting on the sentence "small and large have delimitations," Liu Chuxuan explains: "The large is the Dao. The greatness of the Dao contains Heaven and Earth. The small is the invisible. The discussion of the invisible enters the smallest particles."

10 DZ 1058, 24a. In the same paragraph, Liu Chuxuan also applies the key term of the *Daode jing*, "non-acting" (Chin. *wuwei* 無爲).

11 *Daode jing*, chapter 65. See DZ 664, 1a.

12 The *Taishang laojun kaitian jing* 太上老君開天經 is a hagiography dating from the 6th century that narrates the life of the deified Laozi. This scripture describes the creation of Heaven and Earth as the contrary movements of *qi*, which is imbued with opposing qualities. While the pure *qi* ascends and creates Heaven, the corrupted or turbid *qi* sinks down and creates Earth. In the same text, *Yang* is equated with Heaven and *Yin* with Earth. See DZ 1437 *Taishang laojun kaitian jing*, 2a. The antinomy of purity and corruption plays an important role throughout Liu Chuxuan's commentary as well. While purity coupled with

which the seasonal changes reflect the rising and descending movements of *Yin* and *Yang*. While the rising *Yang* is responsible for the productive cycles that reach their height on the summer solstice, the *Yin* represents the destructive elements in the natural cosmos of later Heaven.[13] Although man wields no influence over those processes, he can base his actions on a thorough examination of them and, in doing so, cultivate a self that reflects the fundamental cosmological notions.

Those who aspire to cultivate their self and attain immortality must first know and understand the secret and paradoxical nature of the "Dao of Heaven". In DZ 1058, Liu Chuxuan explains the term "knowledge" as follows:

> Those who have knowledge that contains the Dao, follow Heaven. Those who have knowledge that does not contain the Dao, follow Man. Follow Heaven – and thus you gain life. Follow Man – and thus you die."

知其有道者順天也。知其無道者順人也。順其天 則人之生也。順其人則人之死也。[14]

In accordance with this application of the fundamental *inner alchemy* theory of reversion, Liu Chuxuan distinguishes two groups of people: The worldly men, who do not understand Heaven and its principles and the enlightened sages or Daoist immortals and perfected men. The worldly men lead an ignorant life. Unaware of Heaven's secret operations they indulge in sinful activities. The sages, however, use their knowledge and wisdom in order to lead a life that accords with celestial principles. The distinction thus refers to two ways of existence that are mutually exclusive and in complete opposition.[15] The different ways of the worldly men and the sages lead in antithetical directions: While the worldly men walk forward and face decay and ultimately death, the sages walk backwards towards life and immortality.[16]

---

quiescence figures as one of the central attributes of the sage's demeanor, corruption characterizes the evil ways of human society.

13 See DZ 122, 4b.
14 DZ 1058, 3b-4a.
15 See DZ 122, 12b: "When the worldly men pursue [the way of] life, the inner nature will return on the road of death. When one attains Dao [on the other hand], he will respect death, and the spirits will travel on the road of life. The Dao and the vulgar [way] and life and death are different roads, and they are mutually exclusive."
16 Underlying this distinction, the reader encounters a traditional motif of religious Daoism. In his commentary, Liu Chuxuan invokes the image of a contemporary society that originated in the proper rules of conduct that the sages of antiquity followed. Hence, Florian C. Reiter translates "contemporaries" instead of "worldly men". See Florian C. Reiter 1997, p.434. Liu Chuxuan's commentary certainly justifies this translation. In my opinion how-

Liu Chuxuan confronts the reader of the commentary with a choice, either practice *Quanzhen* self-cultivation or "walk on the path of death." This choice, the commentary argues, depends on man's ability to understand that his inner nature reflects the macrocosmic principle of the Dao of Heaven in the microcosmic reality of human existence.

Commenting on the "heavenly inner nature of man," Liu Chuxuan argues that every human being is endowed with opposing attributes:

> As for the heavenly inner nature of man, everyone has [the properties of] the good and the evil, the great and the minute, and all that which is desired: The [properties of] civilized and martial, the Dao and the vulgar, the noble and the worthless, the great and the low.[17]

Man is not born with a fate that predestines him to any particular sort of existence. Everyone bears a personal responsibility to avoid acting on the negative aspects of his inner nature and, instead, follow the archetype of the "masters of antiquity who realized the Dao and attained wisdom."

Liu Chuxuan characterizes the "Dao of Heaven" as "ignorant and unknowing". It neither acts intentionally,[18] nor does it show any interest in worldly affairs. It remains entirely impartial in regard to social standing, wealth or accomplishments in the human realm:

> The Dao of Heaven is ignorant and unknowing, but Heaven's mercy is great: Spring is warm, summer is hot, fall is cool and winter is cold. The four seasons transform, they bring forth and complete the ten thousand creatures, and they aid the human world. Those who are prosperous and noble wear illustrious clothes and eat beautiful delicacies. Those who are poor and low [eat] simple foods and [wear] primitive clothes. Everyone as it suits him.[19]

---

ever, Liu Chuxuan's distinction and his use of this term is based on the fundamental *Quanzhen* belief that a proper self-cultivation is impossible if the practitioner is unwilling to renounce the world and live outside the boundaries of the human civilization.

17 In the next section of this chapter, I discuss how the last stage of self-cultivation leads to the eventual dispersal of all opposing qualities. In classical Daoist cosmology, the opposing qualities come into being when Heaven and Earth are created in the processes that lead to the cosmologic state after Heaven. See for example the text DZ 1205 *Santian neijie jing* 三天內解經 from the early 5th century, which relates the opposing qualities of the natural world to Laozi's creation of the cosmos. The first section of this text mentions many of the coupled pairs that Liu Chuxuan's list contains.

18 Generally, in Daoism the actions of the Dao are characterized as *wuwei*. The actions of man however, follow the principle of "intentional action" (Chin. *youwei* 有爲).

19 See DZ 122, 3b-4a.

However, when man does not act in accordance with Heaven, it does eventually recompense. Here, Liu Chuxuan draws on the well-established Daoist theme of celestial retribution for good and evil deeds. He identifies man's improper actions as the true origins of disease and calamities.[20]

Unaware of this fundamental principle, the worldly men cannot predict or prevent a celestial retribution of their sins. Liu Chuxuan does not show any sympathy for the religious activities of his contemporaries. In his eyes, the religiosity of the worldly men who do not submit to the Daoist ideals of *Quanzhen* is only vain and superstitious. Commenting on the sentence "men know the spirits as spirits" he explains:

> The worldly men only know the earthly gods and the Yin-spirits as spirits. Spirits carved in wood and formed from mud are treated as [true] spirits. The foolish do not know that Heaven will send down calamities and sorrows that befit every mistake they make. They kill and harm pigs and lambs, they burn [paper-] money and [paper-] horses, and they pray. When they are sick, they search for peace. When they encounter calamities, they search for good luck.[21]

Even when they participate in religious activities, the attitude of the worldly men remains superficial and their participation does not stem from a thorough understanding of their inner nature or the principles of Heaven. As for the three 'cosmic forces' of Chinese cosmology that I discussed in the third chapter of this study, the worldly men remain in the realm of the Earth and the *Yin*.[22] Their lack of insight into cosmological principles prevents them from apprehending that salvation does not reside in outer activities, but rather in the very self of the human being:

---

20 This is a very old topic and not only in Daoist scriptures. See Florian C. Reiter 1997, p.451. This author relates Liu Chuxan's thoughts on the issue to the *Taiping jing* 太平經. In a footnote on that page, he mentions several papers that address the topic of sin and compensation. The most elaborate explanation of this topic in Liu Chuxuan's commentary appears in DZ 122, 8a-b. For a general description of the content of the *Taiping jing* see Max Kaltenmark, "The Ideology of the *T'ai-p'ing ching*," in: Holmes Welch and Ann Siedel (eds.), *Facets of Taoism*, New Haven 1979, p.19-52. For a thorough study of the concept of sin in the *Taiping jing* see Tsuchiya Masaaki, *Confessions of Sins and Awarness of Self in the Taiping jing*, in: Livia Kohn and Harold D. Roth (eds.), *Daoist Identity: History, Lineage and Ritual*, Hawai 2002, p.39.

21 DZ 122, 8b.

22 The sages, however, belong to Heaven, i.e. the realm of the divine. Heaven is associated with *Yang*. The restoration of primordial *qi* that *Quanzhen* self-cultivation aims for is associated with the ascending movement of *Yang*.

> The worldly men do not know that [their own] self is the mightiest and most sensible being among the ten thousand creatures. The primordial spirits posses a light penetrating Heaven and Earth.[23]

In contrast to the outer and superficial activities of the worldly men, the religiosity of the sage is predicated on an inner attitude that reflects his comprehension of the inner nature of man and fundamental characteristics of Heaven. Since the worldly men do not understand the "impartiality" of Heaven, their actions arise from selfish motivations. The actions of the sage however, whose being reflects both the inner nature of man and Heaven's impartiality, display the greatest virtue and an accordance with celestial principles.

It is noteworthy, that Liu Chuxuan's commentary does not always support the *Quanzhen* idea of a "double cultivation of inner nature and existence" as a simultanuous practice. Instead, cultivation of inner nature has to precede cultivation of existence. For instance, in the following quote Liu Chuxuan provides an explanation of the process of self-cultivation that moves from inner nature to a complete understanding of the two key terms derived from the *Daode jing*:

> The inner nature penetrates existence; existence penetrates Heaven; Heaven penetrates the Dao; and the Dao penetrates thusness. If one internally completes the Dao and externally completes virtue, then this is called wisdom and sainthood.[24]

Inner nature and existence refer to the two-fold self-cultivation of *Quanzhen* Daoism. Cultivating inner nature demands an inner practice. The cultivation of existence refers to proper rules of conduct and the actual behavior of the physical human being in a social world. Hence, inner nature is related to the Dao and existence to virtue. Only a cultivation of both can lead to sainthood and immortality. Liu Chuxuan leaves no doubt that it is only through this double cultivation that the practitioner can attain immortality and, hence, "the road of life." While the above quote may suggest that Liu Chuxuan believed in the primacy of inner cultivation, it is also clear that the outer cultivation of existence remained equally important to him.

In Liu Chuxuan's thought the two-fold self-cultivation is realized in three stages. In the following section I will discuss the three stages of self-cultivation. They are related to the term of the "three vehicles" that appears not only in Liu Chuxuan's texts but also in those written by Wang Chongyang and other masters of early *Quanzhen* Daoism.

---

23 DZ 122, 9b.
24 DZ 122, 4a.

3. The "three vehicles": A narrative of self-cultivation

As I mentioned above, Liu Chuxuan's commentary interprets the three chapters of the *Yinfu jing* as referring to three successive stages of self-cultivation. In his commentary, Liu Chuxuan mentions the term "three vehicles." Coined after the Buddhist term "two vehicles," in Quanzhen it usually designates three different approaches towards self-cultivation.[25] While Liu Chuxuan's commentary does not provide an explication of the three vehicles, a quote from Qiu Chuji illuminates the meaning of the term:

> Those of the highest [vehicle] contemplate the mysterious and meditate, those of the middle [vehicle] chant scriptures and perform rituals, those of the inferior [vehicle] endure hardships, and they do manual labor.[26]

This explanation of the three vehicles corresponds to a passage from Liu Chuxuan's commentary in which he distinguishes three different ranks of men according to their "orifices of the mind."[27] The more orifices with which the mind is endowed, the easier access a person has to the primordial *Yang-qi* mentioned in DZ 244 *Dadan zhizhi*.[28] From Liu Chuxuan's commentary alone, it is impossible to determine if the number of the mind's orifices is naturally limited or if it could be increased by practices of self-cultivation. In DZ 1156 however, Wang Chongyang describes the three vehicles as successive stages of self-cultivation:

> As for the lower vehicle, it is like the newborn child. As for the middle vehicle, it is like the young child sitting on the ground. As for the higher vehicle, it is like the child who walks. If man passes through these three vehicles, he surpasses the three realms.

---

25 Compare Erik Zürcher, *Buddhist Influences on Early Taoism*, in T'oung Pao (ed.), vol. LXVI (1980), p. 115. According to Zürcher, the term occurs incidentally in a multitude of Daoist scriptures without any clear explanation of the precise meaning.

26 See Paulino T. Belamide 2002, p. 131. In DZ 1156, 3b, Wang Chongyang argues that the three vehicles refer to the three chapters of the *Yinfu jing* that are attributed to Laozi in this text.

27 See DZ 122, 6a. Above I argued that Liu Chuxuan's theory does not exclude anyone from self-cultivation in principle. In this passage he mentions those men who do not have orifices of the mind. He calls them "foolish" and does not offer any advice for them.

28 See the second chapter of this study.

下乘者如新生孩兒，中乘者如小兒坐地，上乘者如小兒行走。若人通此三乘便超三界。[29]

In Wang Chongyang's interpretation, the "three vehicles" refer to an educational path. Unlike Qiu Chuji, he stresses the evolutionary character of the "three vehicles." I assume here that Liu Chuxuan's theory is related to the educational path that Wang Chongyang's explanation evokes. This educational path amounts to a gradual opening of the mind's orifices, and the practitioner of *Quanzhen* moves from the lowest group of men to the highest in three successive stages.

But DZ 1156 supports my interpretation in another respect. In this text, Wang Chongyang relates the term "three vehicles" to the three headings of the *Yinfu jing*. Clearly, a quintessential element of early *Quanzhen Daoism* resided in the interpretation of the *Yinfu jing* as describing a threefold cultivation of the self. Liu Chuxuan was influenced by this context and the adoption of this idea reveals the strong impact Wang Chongyang's thought had on Liu Chuxuan. Yet in spite of this, Liu Chuxuan's description of the three stages of self-cultivation is not wholly confined to the three respective chapters of the *Yinfu jing*. Moreover, Liu Chuxuan does not draw any clear demarcation line between the three stages. My description here therefore does not provide an entirely chronological account of his commentary, but instead distills a narrative of self-cultivation in three stages based on the concept of the three vehicles.

The first stage of self-cultivation is largely characterized by the practitioner's retreat from the mundane world. In the second chapter of this study I showed that this retreat was a fundamental demand of early *Quanzhen* ideology and that its description functioned as a central element in the hagiographies devoted to the masters of early *Quanzhen* Daoism. However, Liu Chuxuan does not interpret this retreat primarily as a spatial movement. At a very elementary level of Liu Chuxuan's commentary, retreating denotes refraining from vices and from the evil and corrupted ways of the "worldly men." Here, his commentary differs markedly from Wang Chongyang's respective elaboration of the concept of "leaving the family" in DZ 1233 *Chongyang zhenren lijiao shiwulun*.[30] In Liu's account, neither does the practitioner have to live at the rims of society, nor does he have to dwell in a hut. His commentary indicates that sainthood can even be achieved in an environment that is profoundly alien to it.

In essence, Liu Chuxuan develops a compelling theory of judgment here that draws on Buddhist theory and well-established Daoist ideas. The "worldly man's"

---

29 DZ 1156, 12a.
30 See the second chapter of this study.

faculty of judgment is spoiled by the distractions of the mundane world.³¹ Amidst this world and engaged in sinful patterns of behavior, one cannot see the true reality of the "Dao of Heaven." Refraining from the vices and sins of the mundane world comprises a necessary precondition for the complete liberation of the mind that results in an introspective endeavor. This endeavor in turn leads the practitioner to the proper epistemological distinctions. Commenting on a phrase from the *Yinfu jing*, Liu Chuxuan calls this the "examination of the trigger of the mind." The inner nature of man is endowed with contrary qualities appearing in coupled pairs that reflect the two opposing forces of *Yin* and *Yang*. A thorough examination of his inner nature enlightens the practitioner about those qualities and enables him to choose the *Yang* qualities over the *Yin*. Hence, the practitioner of *Quanzhen* Daoism and eventually the fully realized man distinguishes himself from the worldly men by his use of the "trigger of the mind." While the worldly men would use the trigger for their own profit, the sages would use it in a purely altruistic manner. In DZ 1058, Liu Chuxuan defines the trigger as "wisdom" and explains:

> As for those who do not have the Dao, when they use wisdom they injure men and bring peace to themselves. They are called 'bandits'. As for those who have the Dao, when they use wisdom, they injure themselves and bring peace to men. This is called good fortune.

> 無道之人用智則損於人安其自己。謂之賊也。有道之人用道則損其自己安於人。謂之富也。³²

The practitioner's retreat from the mundane world describes the movement from an outer to an inner reality. When characterizing the outer reality of the mundane world, Liu Chuxuan applies Buddhist terminology. He speaks of "the Gold yoke, the Jade button, the spark from the stone, the lanterns in the wind and the worldly dreams and illusions"³³ that the practitioner must abandon. Epistemologically, this

---

31 See DZ 122, 3a: "I say that the worldly men all hold to the distinctions of high and low [things] they see. The correct can yield the depraved. When there is much depravity, it slanders the correct. As to the depraved methods, my perception is like the light of a firefly." The distinction between "correct" and "depraved methods" refers to the faculty of judgment. Those who are tangled up in mundane activities do not posses the ability to judge things on the basis of the true principles of Heaven.
32 See DZ 1058, 27b. The same notion is expressed in DZ 122, 12b.
33 See DZ 122, 3a. The deluding or empty nature of reality is a fundamental Buddhist notion. In a scripture from the *Tiantai* school, we find the following definition of concentration: "By concentration is meant to know that all dharmas (elements of existence), from the very beginning have no nature of their own. They neither come into or go out of existence.

reality possesses no more value than a dream and could never provide the basis for a proper judgment. The worldly men are thus caught up in a world of erroneous beliefs and deluding images. The inner reality, however, is unspoiled and reflects the true nature of the "Dao of Heaven."

Philosophically speaking, the first stage of self-cultivation leads the practitioner from a process of falsification to a process of verification. First, the practitioner realizes that all his prior beliefs and persuasions were incorrect. Secondly, he replaces his false beliefs with the enlightened notions that are based on a scrutiny of his inner nature. The two ensuing stages of self-cultivation continue this process of verification. Liu Chuxuan's theory of judgment reflects on the paradoxical nature of the "Dao of Heaven". Since it is hidden and impenetrable to the normal consciousness of the "worldly man," his outer perception cannot see the true causes of events. In spite of that, the "Dao of Heaven" pervades everything and informs the human mind as well. Therefore, the practitioner only has to shift his attention from an outer to an inner reality.[34]

In the second stage of self-cultivation, the practitioner adopts the secret patterns of the Dao of Heaven. This adaptation has an outer and an inner aspect. The outer aspect draws on the *Quanzhen* ideology that the true sage leads a life of virtue. The practitioner must practice mercy and good deeds. In doing so, his existence reflects the impartiality of Heaven. Other than the "worldly man" the true sage respects law and the fundamental Confucian moral principles. The practitioner's actions must display the greatest serenity, a serenity he would not abandon even in the face of starvation. The practitioner would always remain calm and continue on his path no matter what obstacles he faces.[35]

This outer attitude, or in the terminology of *Quanzhen*, this cultivation of existence is complemented with a cultivation of inner nature. We have seen that the retreat from the mundane world leads to an inner consciousness. In the second stage of cultivation, this inner consciousness triggers a self-reflective process. When reflecting or meditating on the Dao, the subject of the practitioner's mind is his own self. However, one should not confuse this self with the personality of the "worldly man," whose consciousness is spoiled by his disturbed faculty of judgment. The true self is the self with which the fetus is equipped and whose contamination starts as soon as

---

Because they are caused by illusion and imagination, they exist without real existence." See Wing-Tsit Chan 1973, p.398.

34 See DZ 122, 11b-12a: "And when the vulgar *qi* of the world arrives at the ears, then one is like the deaf. When the thoughts of the Dao arrive at the ears, then one hears."

35 See DZ 122, 8b-9a.

it leaves the mother's womb.³⁶ Essentially, it belongs to the cosmological stage of "former Heaven."³⁷

In describing the correct attitude of the practitioner of *Quanzhen* self-cultivation, Liu again draws heavily on Buddhist terminology.³⁸ However, he integrates this terminology into a framework that remains essentially Daoist. The key concepts employed in his commentary are two Daoist terms that hail from long traditions and appeared first in the *Daode jing*: "Non-acting" (*wuwei* 無為) and "purity and quiescence" (*qingjing* 清靜). Earlier in this chapter, I argued that these concepts describe the actions of the "Dao of Heaven." Consequently, when cultivating his self, the practitioner of *Quanzhen* adopts Heaven's secret patterns of behavior that remain obscured for the "worldly men."

While Liu Chuxuan does not explicitly mention the study of sacred scriptures as a means of self-cultivation, his extensive use of concepts or quotes that derive from scriptures as diverse as the *Daode jing* to the *Jingang jing* (*Diamond Sutra*) highlights the central role such texts played in early *Quanzhen* Daoism. Along with the *Yinfu jing* itself, those scriptures contain the essential truths that the practitioner must realize in the second stage of self-cultivation.

The truths contained in the sacred scriptures guide the practitioner towards recognizing the identity between macrocosmic and microcosmic processes. The practitioner realizes that the very same processes that cause the creational processes in the natural world and the entire universe determine his very existence and body. Those processes are described as the energetic circulation of *qi* and the contrary movements of the emblematic energies of *Yin* and *Yang*. Hence, the truths that the practitioner realizes in the second stage of self-cultivation provide the theoretical framework for the application of inner alchemy. The third stage of self-cultivation consists in the application of this framework.

---

36 Liu Chuxuan's commentary distinguishes between "self," Chin. *ziji* 自己 and "ego," Chin. *wo* 我. The term "self" is related to the positive spiritual aspects of the human being, one's inner nature, one's mind and the "primordial spirits." The "ego," however, is related to the personality of the worldly men. For the term "self" see DZ 122, 9b, for "ego" see DZ 122, 13a.

37 Compare the quote from DZ 244 *Dadan zhizhi* in the first chapter, where the fetus is born with primordial *qi*. Restoring the primordial *qi* is linked to an elaborate description of Daoist cosmology.

38 Liu Chuxuan utilizes the concept of the "four perceptions," which derives from the *Diamond Sutra*, and the Buddhist idea of the "six roots." See DZ 122, 10a. In the same section, Liu Chuxuan equates the Buddha with inner nature.

In the first stage of self-cultivation, the practitioner learns about the proper epistemological distinctions. He realizes the paradoxical character of the Dao through the examination of his inner nature that is endowed with all the cosmological antinomies. The second stage, however, leads to a proper conduct that abandons the negative or *Yin* elements of those antinomies. In the third stage, the application of *inner alchemy*, the practitioner relinquishes the conditional state of posterior Heaven and reverts to the unconditioned state of anterior Heaven. This reversion entails the complete dissolution of all antinomies.

The last section of Liu Chuxuan's commentary is devoted to an esoteric and cryptic description of an *inner alchemy* process that leads the practitioner to a reversion of the natural productive processes and, implicitly, to immortality. As is the case with Ma Danyang's quote on the "regulation of breath," Liu Chuxuan does not explain any specific techniques or practices.[39] Drawing on the symbolic language of *inner alchemy*, Liu Chuxuan explains the reversion of bodily processes triggered by a proper cultivation of the self. It is noteworthy that this reversion appears as a necessary outcome of the practitioner's adaptation of celestial principles. In other words, it is not the result of a conscious endeavor.

The primary quality of the Dao's being is "thusness."[40] This term, often simply translated as naturalness, refers to the unintentional character of the Dao. It describes a pristine and unspoiled state of being that lacks conscious and selfish motivations. The attainment of the Dao primarily consists in the retrogressive abandoning of intentional, conscious and selfish attitudes and their replacement with the "thusness" that characterizes the cosmological state of *anterior Heaven*. Liu Chuxuan relates the central concepts of his commentary to the Dao's unintentional character:

> Thusness, this is the Dao. Purity, this is Heaven. Quiescence, this is Earth. Non-being, this is when inner nature and physical existence are the same body. Action, this is when mercy is exercised and no compensation expected. The creation of the ten thousand creatures and the creation of man are not different. Heaven and Earth let the *qi* circulate, and the material substance becomes thoroughly transformed. When the jade tripod lets lead steam, then the gold-furnace refines mercury.[41]

The actual process of alchemical reversion begins when the practitioner's self-cultivation has reached a stage where the distinctions disappear that make up the physical reality under the condition of *posterior Heaven*. This process entails the "toppling of the five elements" that I mentioned in the first chapter of this study, and it is based on the fundamental notion of the identity between macrocosmic and mi-

---

39 See the second chapter of this study.
40 Chin. *ziran* 自然.
41 DZ 122, 16a.

crocosmic creation. Reverting the normal circulation of *qi* that accords with the cosmological principles of the state after Heaven, the practitioner amalgamates the elixir from his own body and returns to the state of *anterior Heaven*. The process described in this last section of the commentary is mirrored in a passage where Liu describes the bodily processes that lead to an exhaustion of *qi* and hence to death:

> When the inner nature manifests itself in the Yin, then below the kidney-seas and the golden turtle will leak out, and above jade and mercury will disappear from the throat, the *hun*-soul will be lost, the *po*-soul will be dispersed, and the true inner nature will have no owner. If the outer Yin is victorious, the inner Yang declines, the material substance dies and one sinks down [to become] a ghost.[42]

The alchemical processes triggered by the proper cultivation of the self prevent the terminal energetic exhaustion that the "worldly men" face. Eventually, however, the attainment of the Dao or immortality reassembles the pre-cosmological state of "anterior Heaven." The second to last sentence of Liu Chuxuan's commentary explains the eventual outcome of inner alchemy as follows:

> In the total confusion, [the difference] of seclusion and revelation can hardly be estimated.[43]

This cryptic explanation recalls the cosmological state contained in the first passage of the classical Daoist scripture *Taishang laojun kaitian jing*.[44] In this passage, the scripture describes the pre-creational being of the Dao before Laozi created the physical reality as the absence of any antinomies. Before creation, there was no Heaven, no Earth and no Man. None of the coupled pairs that describe the circulation of the opposing forces of *Yin* and *Yang* existed. It is this unconditioned and pre-creational state to which the attainment of Dao leads.

Liu Chuxuan's theory of self-cultivation highlights the fact that early *Quanzhen* pursued a project that was genuinely Daoist in nature. In spite of the Buddhist or Confucian influences on it, Liu Chuxuan's commentary primarily contains basic Daoist ideas. The application of *inner alchemy* that Liu describes rests upon fundamental Daoist cosmological notions that constitute a common ground for a diverse range of schools. The attainment of immortality or sainthood consists of a complete reversion of the natural processes that are described in classical Daoist cosmology. The saint or the immortal achieves a state of being tantamount to the unadorned Dao

---

42 DZ 122, 4b.

43 DZ 122, 16b.

44 The first passage of this text describes the pre-cosmic state of the Dao as follows: "There was no Heaven and there was no Earth. There was no *Yin* and there was no *Yang*. There was no sun and there was no moon. There was no darkness and there was no light. There was no east and there was no west. […] There was no birth and there was no deceasing." See DZ 1437 *Taishang laojun kaitian jing* 太上老君開天經, 1a.

under the condition of the cosmological state of *anterior Heaven*. Below the surface of Liu Chuxuan's highly complex and eclectic commentary, readers encounter themes and ideas that were already contained in ancient Daoist scriptures such as the *Daode jing* or the *Zhuangzi*.

Conclusion

The primary goal of this study was to explore the three main foundations of Liu Chuxuan's theory of self-cultivation: The theory of inner alchemy used in his commentary, the Daoist school of *Quanzhen* and the transmission of sacred scriptures, here epitomized in the *Yinfu jing*. In the first chapter I focused on two central aspects of *inner alchemy*. Both the theory of reversion and the practice of circulating and restoring *qi* play a crucial role in Liu Chuxuan's commentary. The topics I discussed in the second chapter shed light on Liu Chuxuan's affiliation with early *Quanzhen* Daoism. My discussion of his hagiographies helped illuminate Liu Chuxuan's personality and showed how the authors of the hagiographies attempted to re-interpret his life in the context of fundamental *Quanzhen* ideas. Many core elements of *Quanzhen* ideology that I discussed in that chapter appear throughout Liu Chuxuan's commentary. The third chapter concentrated on the pivotal role classical scriptures such as the *Yinfu jing* played in early *Quanzhen* Daoism. In the last chapter, I explained the two central themes in Liu Chuxuan's commentary, the concept of the "Dao of Heaven" and the narrative of self-cultivation as a process that leads man from his ignorant life amidst the mundane world to immortality and sainthood. In this narrative, Liu Chuxuan draws heavily on the current of inner alchemy. He uses the symbolic language of *inner alchemy*, and the final stage of refinement found in his commentary epitomizes this theory. The commentary also reveals that Liu Chuxuan possessed a vast knowledge of the general Daoist legacy. In many passages he quotes sacred Daoist scriptures and classical commentaries such as the *Heshang gong* commentary on the *Daode jing*. Hence, this study supports the assumption that *Quanzhen* was intrinsically Daoist despite its eclectic character.

Liu Chuxuan's commentary is a typical example of early *Quanzhen* literature for three reasons: 1.) Both in style and content, his commentary is eclectic and makes use of concepts and notions derived from the "three teachings"; 2.) His theory of self-cultivation insists on the "double cultivation of inner nature and existence"; 3.) He insists that self-cultivation entails both an outer practice of virtue and an inner practice of Dao.

Nonetheless, Liu Chuxuan's commentary does not always accord with the teachings of Wang Chongyang and his other disciples. Unlike the 'mainstream' of early *Quanzhen* Daoism, Liu Chuxuan is not convinced that a retreat from society necessarily implies a spatial movement that leads away from the mundane world. In his understanding, retreat primarily refers to a spiritual attitude that can be attained in any environment. Another difference is that some passages of his commentary indicate his inclination towards a cultivation of inner nature. While he generally supports the idea of a "double cultivation," in his commentary the cultivation of inner nature tends to take precedence. Moreover, it is from the cultivation of inner nature that all practice originates.

As I argued in the preface, one of the central features of early *Quanzhen* was the heterogeneous composition of the group of the seven perfected. Liu Chuxuan's commentary lends support to the assumption that *Quanzhen* was a much more heterogeneous movement in its beginnings than it is today. This heterogeneous character of the movement is also reflected in the history *a posteriori* that the hagiographies of early *Quanzhen* narrate. The individuality of Wang Chongyang and the group of the seven perfected is present both in the hagiographic texts and in their literary legacy. While most differences may seem minor, they reveal that in its early days *Quanzhen* Daoism was not a highly organized religion.

Although dealing with a medieval Daoist text, this study may also be valuable for scholars interested in modern China. *Quanzhen* is, as illuminated in the introduction, a living religion, and Liu Chuxuan is one of the most sacred figures in its teachings. His commentary may not be known outside the confines of *Quanzhen* Daoism, but the ideas it contains still affect everyday life in China. The *inner alchemy* theory of early *Quanzhen* Daoism sheds light on a broader current in religious Daoism that has evolved into such contemporary practices of self-cultivation as modern *Qigong*. A thorough study of more recent texts in the Daoist tradition might reveal the ways in which Liu Chuxuan's ideas influenced later masters of *Quanzhen*, as well as contemporary practices or techniques that pursue similar macrobiotic goals.

Commentary on The Yellow Emperor's Scripture of the Hidden Contracts[1]

Commented by Liu Chuxuan, the master Changsheng.

The upper chapter: The spirit immortal embraces the One: on the Dao[2]

To perceive the Dao of Heaven and to grasp the phases of Heaven[3] – this is all. (DZ 122.1a-2a)

To perceive:
This means that the five eyes are shining radiantly. One lets the eye of Heaven shine, the eye of intelligence, the eye of law, the eye of the Dao and the eye of the spirit.[4]

---

1 DZ 122 *Yinfu jing zhu* 陰符經註.
2 My translation of the quotations from the *Huangdi Yinfu jing* (hereafter *Yinfu jing*) owes much to Christopher. C. Rand's translation of the respective scripture. However, since Christopher C. Rand's interpretation of the *Yinfu jing* as a military treatise does not always suit my purposes here, I had to make some significant changes. Clearly, Liu Chuxuan's commentary understands the *Yinfu jing* as a metaphysical essay focusing on questions of enlightenment and wisdom. For Christopher C. Rand's translation see Christopher. C. Rand, *Li Ch'uan and Chinese Military Thought*, in: *Harvard Journal of Asiatic Studies*, vol. 39, issue 1 (Jun., 1979), p. 107 – p. 137. A more popular translation of the *Yinfu Jing* can be found in Thomas Cleary, *Vitality, Energy, Spirit, A Taoist Sourcebook*, Boston and London, 1991, p. 220 – 222, and an early translation in John Legge, *The Texts of Taoism*, New York 1959, p. 697 – 706. Cleary's translation is part of a complete translation of the commentary on the *Yinfu jing* written by the *Qing*-dynasty Daoist Liu Yiming. John Legge's translation adds extensive annotations.
3 Chin. *xing* 行. The word *xing*, lit. "to walk" or "to practice", is related to the concept of *wuxing* 五行, the five transformational phases or elements, which plays an important role throughout the *Yinfu jing* and Liu Chuxuan's entire commentary. The theory of the five elements is also one of the main sources of *neidan*-literature in general. See the first chapter of this study.

When the five beams [of these eyes] are bright and penetrating, then the five *skandhas*[5] return into the void, and one sees that Dao of Heaven.

Within Heaven there is yet another Heaven. It is the Heaven of pure *qi*,[6] which is above Earth. At its greatest height this Heaven reaches up 84,000 miles.

In the human body, everyone receives the one *qi* of Heaven. There is strong *qi*, and there is weak *qi*. When it is [well] blended and harmonious, then it gives birth to sagacious and saintly people. When this *qi* is inverted and dispersed, then one sinks down and becomes a ghost.

Dao:
It is outside of Heaven, Earth and the ten thousand creatures, the body of the void and non-being. In the human body one can catch a glimpse of it. This completely depends on an emptied mind. Then the highest inner nature[7] and the Dao will be in

---

4 The concept of the *five eyes* is originally Buddhist. However, Liu Chuxuan's list given here differs from the Buddhist collection. In Buddhism, the *five eyes* are the eye of the flesh, the eye of Heaven, the eye of intelligence, the eye of the law and the eye of the Buddha. See *Ciyuan*, Beijing 1998, p.74.
5 The five *skandhas* are "the components of an intelligent being, especially a human being." In detail, the list contains form or matter, Chin. *se*色; sensation or feeling, Chin. *shou*受; conception or discerning, Chin. *xiang*想; the processing of mind, Chin. *xing*行; mental faculty of perception and cognition, Chin. *shi*識. See W.A. Soothill and L. Hodous, *A Dictionary of Chinese Buddhist Terms* (repr.), Richmond, 1995, p. 126a.
6 There is no direct equivalent for the Chinese word *qi*氣 in any western language. Its literal meaning is breath, but especially in the Daoist context it should instead be understood as a ubiquitous energy arising from the Dao and informing all living beings.
7 Chin. *xing*性, here translated as "inner nature," and chin. *ming*命, here translated as " existence," are complementary concepts in inner alchemy. For both terms, there is a variety of translations and interpretations in Western literature. Although no translation will be completely satisfying, I chose mine carefully. Generally speaking, *xing* refers to the spiritual aspects of a human being, whereas *ming* clearly refers to the material or physical person existing in a social world. One of the more literal meanings of *ming* is "fate" or "mandate" as in "mandate of Heaven," Chin. *tianming*天命. In inner alchemy, *xing* is often associated with the spirits, Chin. *shen*神, while *ming* may stand for *qi*. In his commentary, Liu Chuxuan also argues in this way: "The inner nature (*xing*), that is the spirit." See my translation below. And in the text *Chongyang zhenren shou danyang ershisi jue* 重陽真人授丹陽二十四訣 (*Twenty-four Instructions Wang Chongyang Bestowed to Ma Danyang*, DZ 1158, 1b) the founder of *Quanzhen*-Daoism Wang Chongyang answers Ma Danyang's question about the two terms *xing* and *ming* in the following fashion: "*Xing*, that is the original spirit. *Ming*, that is the original *qi*. And the name [for both] is *xing* and *ming*."

harmony with each other. He who grasps this will guard perfection and will not be false, he will realize that which is correct and not depraved.

Heaven:
The sentence "Heaven gives birth" is related to the ten thousand creatures. Heaven gives birth to the ten thousand creatures, it bears and completes them, but it does not harvest, and it does not take from them. It supports the ten thousand people of the ten directions and the three realms,[8] but it also does not expect any compensation from them. It only wants all living beings to realize the principles of the Dao of Heaven in a complete and enlightened way. It wants man not to hate and not to love in his ten thousand activities and to be evenly balanced like Heaven. Those who belong to the human realm have sentiments; but those who understand Heaven have no sentiments.[9] And this is the compensation for the mercy of Heaven. If one is not in accord with the principles of Heaven, pursues the corrupt, the evil, the depraved and the licentious, he will suffer from many diseases, die an early death and sink down into the hell of earth.[10] When enough hardships have been endured, he will be reborn as an animal, and he will lose the human body.

If one is in accord with the Dao of Heaven and is always virtuous, then the *qi* will be in harmony. If one is always pure, then he lets shine the inner nature. If one

---

One of the main and distinctive features of *Quanzhen*-Daoism is that its proponents insist on the so-called *dual cultivation of xing and ming*. Nonetheless, Liu Chuxuan's commentary on the *Yinfu jing* is not always clear in this respect. In some of his elaborate explanations, it seems that he favors the cultivation of *xing* over the cultivation of *ming*.

8 Chin. *shifangsanjie*十方三界. According to traditional Daoist thought, the universe consists of ten directions and three realms. The "ten directions" are east, north, south, west, northeast, southeast, southwest, northwest, up and down. The "three realms" refer to the realm of Heaven, the realm of Earth and the realm of [the element] water. The term "three realms" may also refer to the realm of the infinite, the realm of the highest pole and the realm of reality; or to the realm of desire, the realm of colors and the realm of the uncolored respectively. These concepts are borrowed from Buddhism. See ZHDJDCD, p. 489 and Erik Zürcher, *Buddhist Influence on Early Taoism*, p. 118.

9 The bad influences that human sentiments can exercise on man are a topic throughout the commentary. Compare Liu Chuxuan's elaborate explanation of this term in DZ 1058 *Wuwei changshen zhenren zhizhen yulu*無爲清精長生真人至真語錄, 28b: "As for the sentiments – they are crooked. Hence, the inner nature of the Dao has no sentiments, but it seems that the body has its sentiments. If one controls [the sentiments], then the inner nature of the Dao has sentiments but the body seems to have no sentiments."

10 Chin. *diyu*地獄.

always forgets the sentiments, then he will guard his own existence.[11] If one is always without contamination,[12] then he will be enlightened about the Dao. If one never breaks the regulations of Heaven, then there will be no sins. One does not cultivate worldly fortunes, but embraces the Dao and completes his true (perfect) fortune. One is not obstructed by wrong-headed schools and minor methods,[13] but will suddenly understand the [concept of] non-acting[14] and the ten thousand methods. And therefore, any adherence to the three realms will be overcome.

Heaven has five bandits, and he who sees them will be brilliant. (DZ 122.2a-b)

Heaven has five bandits:[15]
There are no [real] bandits in Heaven. They (the bandits) are not the thieves and the bandits of this world, and they are not the six bandits of man.[16] But they are extraordinary bandits. Heaven has the correct *qi* of the five directions. Within the human body, they become the mothers of the spirits.[17] In the twelve hours of the heavenly

---

11 Chin. *ming*命. See also fn. 7 in this chapter for an explanation of my translation of this term.
12 The mind can be contaminated, Chin. *ran*染, with desires and sexual passions. The concept can also refer to a state of impurity. See W. E. Soothill, p. 304b.
13 Chin. *bangmen*傍門. This expression also appears in *Huangdi yinfujing zhu* 7b where it refers to an inferior epistemic state in which the mind has not yet abandoned the so-called "four perceptions", chin. *sixiang* 四相, a concept diriving from Buddhism. See my translation below.
14 Chin. *wuwei* 無為.
15 Most commentaries on the *Yinfu jing* agree that the *five bandits* are the five elements. Compare for instance DZ 121 *Huangdi yinfu jing zhu*, 1.3b: "The meaning of the 'five bandits' is the five elements." Ma Danyang recommends this commentary on the *Yinfu jing* in DZ 1052 *Danyang zhenren yulu, 10a*. Therefore, we may assume that Liu Chuxuan was familiar with it.
16 The "six bandits of man," Chin. *liuzei*六賊, are the six evil influences that disturb the cultivation of the Dao: the colors, the sounds, the odors, the tastes, the feelings of touch and the law or the method. See *ZHDJDCD*, p.473.
17 In DZ 121 *Huangdi yinfu jing*, 1b another commentary on the *Yinfujing* by the Daoist Tang Chun and popular among masters of early *Quanzhen* Daoism, we find the following explanation: "The spirit is the son of the *qi*; and the *qi* is the mother of the spirit." The relationship between *qi* and spirit Liu Chuxuan envisions is clearly productive. *Qi* is the

cycle,[18] [the *qi*] draw [from each other] and supplement [each other].[19] They revolve and circulate. The supreme subtlety[20] is infinite. About this it is said that Heaven and Earth are within the non-being. The flourishing *qi* of Yin and of Yang give birth among the ten thousand creatures.

Man eats the five [kinds of] grains in order to nourish his physical form.[21] The vanities and the dust of this world [let man] sink into [the elements] water and fire. Within the human body the essences of the five [kinds of] grains are preserved, and they shape[22] the existence. If one has existence and attains the inner nature, he lasts. If one has inner nature and attains existence, he has longevity. As to existence, it is the dark turtle of the northern Sea.[23] Always embracing it, the old Ding[24] completed the physical form. As for the five bandits, they are the True Yang. The True Yang of Heaven recognizes the True Yin.[25] The five bandits steel the treasures of the northern Sea.

---

ubiquitous energy informing the macrocosm which in turn in the microcosmic reality of the human body produces the spirit, one of the "three treasures" in *inner alchemy*.

18   The term "Heavenly cycle," lit. *"orbiting Heaven"*, Chin. *zhoutian*周天, is commonly used in literature concerned with inner alchemy, Chin. *neidan*內丹. It refers to the time-cycles and periods of exercises. It also refers to the circulation of the essences, Chin. *jing* 精, the *qi*氣 and the spirits, Chin. *shen*神, in the body. See *ZHDJDCD*, p. 1199.

19   The term "draw and supplement," Chin. *choutian*抽添, is a technical term in inner alchemy. Traditionally, it refers to the process of refining lead and mercury, the two most important substances in both the cultivation of the internal elixir and the cultivation of the external elixir.

20   Chin. *zhimiao*至妙.

21   Chin. *xing*形. This term generally denotes physical beings but also more specifically the human body.

22   Lit. "make," Chin. *wei*爲.

23   The "turtle of the northern sea," Chin. *beihai zhi gui*北海之龜, here "the dark turtle of the northern sea," Chin. *beihai zhi wugui* 北海之烏龜, is a metaphorical name for the kidneys. In inner alchemy, the kidneys are believed to be the seat of the physical existence (*ming*). The kidneys contain the true Yang, Chin. *zhenyang*真陽, the primordial Yin, Chin. *yuanyin*元陰 and the essences, Chin. *jing*精, have their origin in the kidneys, too. See *Daojiao dacidian*, Beijing 1994, p.370 and p. 634.

24   I could not find this term in any other related texts. Originally, the term refers to an herb. In the pharmacological tractate DZ 768 *Tujing yi bencao*, 2.30a, the term is identified with an herb known as *Tongcao*通草.

25   The term "True Yin" refers to the central line of the trigram *li*, as the term "True Yang" refers to the central line of the trigram *kun*. Since the trigram *li* is composed of two unbroken Yang-lines embracing a single broken Yin-line, the True Yin is also referred to as the

He who protects those treasures will be brilliant. This is how the ten thousand creatures are the thieves of man.

The five bandits are in the mind. They are actuated in Heaven. The universe is in the hand, and the ten thousand transformations arise within the body. (DZ 122.2b-3b)

The five bandits are in the mind:
This sentence means that the five elements topple.[26] If they are in the mind, then the True [element] water[27] will rise. If they are adversely[28] [ordered], then the orifices of the mind will not be opened. The kidney-water will run down, and one walks on the path of death. The worldly men have not attained the Dao of the saints. And all men who do not practice[29] the Dao are like this. The masters of antiquity who realized the Dao and who attained wisdom were completely different.

"Yin inside the Yang". Analogously, the trigram *kun* consists of an upper and a lower broken Yin-line and an unbroken Yang-line in the center. Thus, the True Yang is also referred to as the "Yang inside the Yin". Fabricio Pregadio points out that as early as in the *Zhouyi Cantong qi* – a central source of reference for *neidan*-literature – True Yin and True Yang are associated with lead and mercury respectively. See *ZHDJDCD*, p.1220, and Fabricio Pregadio, *Inner Alchemy (neidan)*, in: Livia Kohn (ed.), *Daoist Handbook*. Leiden, Boston and Köln, 2000, p. 466.

26 Chin. *diandao* 顛倒, „topple" or "turn upside down", is a technical term commonly used in *neidan*-literature. Traditional Chinese cosmology distinguishes between a state "before Heaven", Chin. *xiantian*先天, and "after Heaven", Chin. *houtian*後天. During the cosmogonic process, Yang ascends and becomes Heaven, and Yin descends and forms Earth. When the five elements topple, this order is overthrown, and thus one will be able to revert to the cosmogonic phase referred to as the former Heaven. See *Daojiao dacidian*, Beijing, 1994, p. 234 and the first chapter of this study.

27 The term "True water," Chin. *zhenshui* 真水, refers to the *qi* arising in the kidneys. This *qi* contains "True water". See *Daojiao dacidian*, Beijing 1994, p.793.

28 Chin. *ni*逆. Usually the term *ni* ("to rebel," "to act against," "to revert") has a very positive meaning in inner alchemy. It refers to the process of reversing the usual course of nature, one of the central goals of inner alchemy. Here, however it is used for those who do not let the five elements topple and who are, indeed, in accord with the normal course of nature.

29 Literally, the word for "practice" means "walk," Chin. *xing*行. Analogously to the sentence before, we can read this sentence as "And all men who do not walk on the Dao are like this."

I say that the worldly men all hold to the distinctions of high and low [things] they see. The correct can yield the depraved. When there is much depravity, it slanders the correct. As to the depraved methods, my perception is like the light of a firefly.

The correct Dao [on the other hand] has the radiance of the sun and the moon. Even when the night is dark and the radiance is feeble, it is still revealing like the radiance of the sun and the moon. It plainly illuminates the ten directions and the three realms. Is this like seeing the light of a firefly? The saints grasp the universe, Yin and Yang mutate thoroughly, and Heaven and Earth unite in Peace.[30]

The ten thousand transformations arise within the body:
The ten thousand transformations complete the physical form.[31] Among the ten thousand creatures, it is only the one being man who arrives at greatness and nobility. Snatching the creational process and internally cultivating the body outside the body[32] - this is called "attaining the Dao." One penetrates the ten thousand transformations, saves the creatures outside, has compassion with all living beings, realizes the Gold yoke, the Jade button[33], the spark from the stone, the lanterns in the wind[34]

---

30 Chin *tai*泰. Tai is one of the sixty-four hexagrams of the *Yi jing*, the Book of Changes. The theory of inner alchemy draws heavily on the theory elucidated in the Book of Changes, and Liu Chuxuan's commentary is no exception here. The hexagram related to the character *tai* is composed of one trigram *kun* above and one trigram *qian* below. The trigram *kun* is associated with Earth, whereas the trigram *qian* symbolizes Heaven. Hence, in one of the classic commentaries we find: "The small goes, the great comes, and auspicious signs pervade. Heaven and Earth exchange [their positions], and the ten thousand creatures communicate." See the first chapter of this study.
31 Chin. *xing*形
32 Chin. *shenwai zhishen*身外之身. In inner alchemy, the "body outside the body" refers to the spiritual body of a person who has cultivated the Dao or the inner elixir. It is also known as the "holy body" or the "true body", Chin. *fashen*法身, a term derived from Buddhism that also occurs in Wang Chongyang's cultivation text *chongyang lijiao shiwulun* 重陽立教十五論 (*Wang Chongyang sets forth his teachings in fifteen discourses*, DZ 1233, 5b). See Sing Chow Wu, *A Study of the Taoist Internal Elixir – its Theory and Development*, PhD-dissertation, New York 1973, p.132.
33 In Buddhism, the 'gold yoke', Chin. *jinjia*金加, and the 'jade button,' Chin. *yuniu*玉扭, are metaphors for worldly attachments that lead to endless suffering. In DZ 1141 *Xianle ji* 仙樂集, 4.13b, Liu Chuxuan explains: "Girls are the gold yoke and the sentiments of love are the jade buttons."
34 These metaphors refer to the fleeting and impermant nature of the world.

and the worldly dreams and illusions.³⁵ One stands away from corruption and the evil, but gets close to purity and the good. Externally one is in harmony with the human way, and internally one follows the true guidance of the Highest Lord Lao and the Patriarch-Buddha.³⁶ And then the ten thousand *dharmas* reverse into the One.³⁷ One may be in the midst of the worldly affairs, but the inner nature rises like the lotus³⁸ from the water.

This is called "completing one's virtue." It is the enlightenment the highest immortals achieved about the ten thousand transformations.

The inner nature of Heaven is man, and the mind of man is the triger.³⁹ By establishing the Dao of Heaven, man is firmly based. (DZ 122.3b-4a).

As to the heavenly inner nature of man, everyone has [the properties of] the good and the evil,⁴⁰ the great and the minute, and all that which is desired: The [properties

---

35 I.e. the delusional character of the world.
36 Chin. *taishang zufo*太上祖佛. This is a contraction of the sacred name of Laozi, *taishang laojun* and a name of the Buddha known in the *Chan*-school of Buddhism that had a strong influence on the *Quanzhen*-school. Liu Chuxuan probably refers to the old *huahu*-legend, according to which it was Laozi himself who first appeared as the Buddha and created Buddhism. For an exhaustive account of this legend see Florian C. Reiter, *Leben und Wirken Lao-Tzu's in Schrift und Bild Lao-chün-pa-shih-i-t'u-shuo*, Würzburg 1990, p. 11 – 12 and p. 34. Also see Livia Kohn, *God of the Dao*, Ann Arbor 1998, p.275-89.
37 The term "ten thousand beings", Chin. *wanfa*萬法, is derived from Buddhism. It refers to "everything that has noumenal or phenomenal existence." See Soothill, p. 412a.
38 The lotus plays an important role in the metaphorical language of *Quanzhen* because it signifies purity arising from a corrupt and dirty environment. It appears in the titles of two collections of *Quanzhen* hagiographies and in the name of one of the religious societies that Wang Chongyang established in Shandong.
39 Chin. *ji*機. In DZ 1058,29b, Liu Chuxuan equates this term with wisdom: "The 'trigger' – that is wisdom. When a man who does not have the Dao uses wisdom, he injures men [in order to] bring peace to his self. Those [men] are called bandits. A man who has the Dao, he injures his self and brings peace to men. This is called good fortune."
40 In DZ 1058, 4b, Liu Chuxuan gives the following explanation for the word 'good' (Chin. *shan*善): "'Good' is when the square is rounded and the crooked is straightened. One adapts to the material substance and is in accordance with man. And when one does not produce the ten thousand evils, this is called the true good." In the same text, 4b – 5a, he

of] civilized and martial, the Dao and the vulgar, the noble and the worthless, the great[41] and the low. As to the inner nature of man, from antiquity until today, [man] is thrown into the womb, changes his skin [like an insect], sells his bones and changes his shape like an ant. He circulates and has not even temporarily arrived at the trigger of the mind yet. Each of the ten thousand daily mutations contains [the properties of] the clever and the dull, the correct and the depraved, the deep and the shallow, the wide and the narrow, the long and the short, the benevolent and the malevolent, the pure and the corrupt, the virtuous and the foolish, love and hatred, being and non-being. If one examines the trigger of the mind, then he understands the inner nature of man.

Establishing the Dao of Heaven:
The Dao of Heaven is ignorant[42] and unknowing, but Heaven's mercy is great: Spring is warm, summer is hot, fall is cool and winter is cold. The four seasons transform, they bring forth and complete the ten thousand creatures, and they aid the human world.

Those who are prosperous and noble wear illustrious clothes and eat beautiful delicacies. Those who are poor and low [eat] simple foods and [wear] primitive clothes. Everyone as it suits him.

The Dao rises in the material things, and by distributing the raw substance it forms vessels.[43] They adorn the human realm like flowers, and like embroidery they are the ten thousand people's joy and pleasure.

---

explains the term 'evil' as follows: "'Evil' is when man is not virtuous. When man is not in accordance with Heaven, then Heaven is not in accordance with man."

41 In the same text, Liu Chuxuan discusses the terms 'great': "Those who attained greatness and hid their highness thus transformed their sainthood." (DZ 1058,7a).

42 Chin. *yu* 愚. The word *yu* also appears in the list of properties ascribed to the daily transformations and below in the *Yinfu jing* where it refers to those who are not in accord with the Dao of Heaven. While its meaning is clearly negative in those contexts, here it refers to a positive aspect of Heaven's nature that can also be found in the impartiality of Heaven, which the *Yinfu jing* discusses below. Being ignorant and unknowing, the Dao of Heaven is completely impartial and it is not involved in the affairs of the ordinary secular world. In DZ 1058, 5b, Liu Chuxuan explains the meaning of the term: "'As for 'ignorance' – the men of antiquity who achieved greatness distanced themselves from the delusions of the world, and their outer appearance was ignorant."

43 Here, Liu Chuxuan uses a slightly changed quote from the *Daode jing*. The *Daode jing* has "The raw substance is distributed, and thus it forms vessels," Chin. *pu san ze wei qi* 朴散則爲器. Chin. *pu* 朴, lit. "uncarved wood," refers to the Dao or the utmost principle of creation, whereas Chin. *qi* 氣 here refers to the physical world. The concept of the productive relationship between Dao and *qi* is more ancient than the *Daode* jing. It departs from the *xici* commentary on the Book of Changes, Chin. *Zhouyi* 周易 or *Yijing* 易經: "That

By establishing the Dao of Heaven man is firmly based:
The wise men are enlightened about the principles of the Dao of Heaven. Secretly they practice the Dao of Heaven. They do not speak [about it], but yet they are wise. They are in accord with the common virtues, but yet they do not let the people know. They spread happiness, but yet they do not expect any compensation from man. If man walks on the Dao of Heaven in accord with this, then it is its [Heaven's] virtue by which man is supported firmly.

The interior [being of man] cherishes an intelligence of penetrating [strength]. Man should realize all the ten thousand transformations and penetrate all the ten thousand methods. [And then] there will be no partiality in the ten thousand creatures, and no contamination will arise from the ten thousand transformations.

The inner nature penetrates[44] existence; existence penetrates Heaven; Heaven penetrates the Dao; and the Dao penetrates thusness.[45] If one internally completes the Dao and externally completes virtue, then this is called wisdom and sainthood.

---

which has form and is supreme is called Dao; that which has form and is inferior is called *qi*." See ZHDJCD, p. 439.

44 The Chinese word *tong*通, which is widely used throughout Liu Chuxuan's commentary, has a variety of meanings. It can have the meaning "to communicate," but also "to penetrate," "to understand," "to circulate" or "to go/to pass through." However, my translation corresponds with Zhang Guangbao's interpretation. He comments on this passage of Liu Chuxuan's text: "The commentary of the *Yinfu jing* also stresses the mutual connections of inner nature (*xing*) and physical existence (*ming*). [...] The existence penetrates the inner nature just as the element water and the element fire recognize each other. The inner nature penetrates the existence just like the element earth and the element water recognize each other." See Zhang Guangbao, *Jinyuan quanzhendao neidan xinxinglun yanjiu*, Taibei 1992, p. 92.

45 Chin. *ziran*自然. The Chinese term is often translated as 'nature.' Literally, it refers to an unaffected and pristine state of being. The 25th chapter of the *Daode jing* explains: "Man is ruled by Earth, Earth is ruled by Heaven, Heaven is ruled by the Dao and the Dao is ruled by thusness." The *Heshang gong* commentary interprets this phrase as follows: "The inner nature of the Dao is thusness. It is not ruled by anything else." See DZ 664 *Daode zhenjing*, 7a and DZ 682 *Daode zhenjing zhu*, 21b.

Heaven releases the trigger of death, and the dragons and the snakes arise from the ground. Man releases the trigger of death, and Heaven and Earth turn around, over and over. (DZ 122.4a-5a)

Heaven releases the trigger of death:
It is the warm pole that then turns into coolness. The coolness turns into the winds of [the element] metal,[46] and the [element] metal turns into cold *qi*.[47] In ten thousand [parts the element] wood falls and scatters, decays and disperses. The dragons coil up in the vast sea, the snakes hibernate in a deep cave. On the winter solstice,[48] the one yang rises, and gradually it brings forth the harmonious *qi*. When spring arrives, the ten thousand creatures sprout. The dragons and the snakes rise from their hibernation in the ground.

Man releases the trigger of death:
It is the inner nature of man, which is the magic light of the Pure Yang.[49] All [the sentiments of] love and desire residing in the human mind arise from the being of the ten thousand creatures of the world. One lusts for the *burning cottage*,[50] affectionate love, one struggles for fame and competes for profits, one is lost in wine, sensuality, wealth and anger.[51] Every kind of pleasure and love displays this at any

---

46 In traditional Chinese thought, the element metal, Chin. *jin*金, is associated with the season autumn and the direction west. Thus, here we could also translate as "west wind" or "autumn winds."
47 Chin. *shuoqi*朔氣.
48 The winter solstice, Chin. *dongzhi*冬至, is the 22nd of the 24 solar terms and marks an important day in the traditional Chinese lunar calendar. It also refers to the shortest day of the solar year. For a description of the rituals performed on this holiday see Michael Saso, *Taoism and the Rite of Cosmic Renewal*, Washington: Washington State University Press, p.39. In DZ 1058, 6a, Liu Chuxuan explains the relationship between summer solstice and winter solstice: "On the summer solstice the *Yin* is born; on the winter solstice the *Yang* is born."
49 Chin. *chunyang*純陽.
50 The 'burning cottage' is a Buddhist term that refers to sensual desires.
51 "Wine, sensuality, wealth and anger," Chin *jiusecaiqi*酒色財氣, is an expression that commonly occurs in the writings of the founder of the *Quanzhen*-school, Wang Chongyang. It denotes the seductive elements in secular life. For example, in the instructional manual *Chongyang jiaohuaji* (DZ 1154, 2.3a) we find: "Every man who wants to cultivate the Dao first has to be in accordance with these 24 characters and abandon *wine, sensuality, wealth and anger*." And in the cultivation text DZ 1156, 1a *Chongyang zhenren jinguan yusuo jie*重陽真人金關玉鎖誡 (*Instructions on the Golden Pass and the Jade Lock*

point of time. The desires and sentiments one constantly has in mind all belong to the Yin. When the inner nature manifests itself in the Yin, then below the kidney-seas and the golden turtle will leak out, and above jade and mercury will disappear from the throat, the *hun*-soul will be lost, the *po*-soul[52] will be dispersed, and the true inner nature will have no owner. If the outer Yin is victorious, the inner Yang declines, the material substance dies and one sinks down [to become] a ghost.

But if man is suddenly enlightened about the highest Dao, he realizes and penetrates the being of the ten thousand creatures. And this is called "the Yang kills the Yin". The inner nature will [then] be as clear as the bright moon, and the mind will be pure like Heaven ten thousand miles without clouds, the radiance of thusness will reveal the ten thousand appearances in a glorious way.

Man releases the trigger of death:
[When this happens, man] completely disperses the entire Yin, spontaneously the *hun*-soul will be pure, and the *po*-soul will be quiescent. And Yin and Yang topple.

Heaven and Earth topple over and over:
The creational process bears and completes the three elixirs, and they congeal and arise out of the skin and shell of Heaven and Earth.
[And thus] the physical form reveals the true body outside the body.[53]

---

by the Perfected Chongyang) Wang Chongyang answers the question after the "subtle principles of the cultivation of perfection" in the following fashion: "The first [principle] is to abandon the nameless vexations. The second [principle] is to give up desires, affectionate love, *wine, sensuality, wealth and anger*."

52 The *hun*魂 and the *po*魄 are two different kinds of souls that each human being possesses. The *hun* reside in the heart and are thought to be the physiological equivalent of *shen*神, the celestial spirits. The *po*-souls, on the other hand, are located in the kidneys. While the *hun*-souls easily and frequently leave the body and report to Heaven, the *po*-souls "deliberately aim to destroy us. They are the spirits of the skeleton, that which is heaviest in the human body, most earthbound. This close tie to the earth makes it difficult for them to tolerate the authority of the higher spirits. They try by every means to free themselves in order to rejoin their natural environment – to enable the skeleton to return to earth. It is, therefore, the job of the director-spirits (*shen, hun*) to dominate, discipline, and contain them." See Kristofer Schipper, *The Taoist Body*, Taibei 1994 (reprint), p. 36.

53 Chin. *shenwai zhenshen*身外真身. See fn. 32 of this chapter for an explanation of the related term "body outside the body."

When Heaven and man release in harmony, the ten thousand transformations have a stable basis. (DZ 122.5a-b)

Heaven and man:
The inner nature of man penetrates Heaven. When they release in harmony, the mind exhausts the material substance. If man thoroughly understands the worldly dream of the human realm he will understand and know that blooming and wilting, grace and disgrace, victory and defeat, prosperity and calamities, happiness and sadness, life and death – [that all these] are the eternal affairs from antiquity until today. If man communicates with the principles of Heaven, he will truly blossom, and he will not wilt; he will truly be graceful, and he will not be disgraceful; he will truly be victorious, and he will not be defeated; he will truly prosper, and he will not [endure] any calamities; he will [experience] true happiness, and he will not [experience] sadness; he will truly live, and he will not die. And this is enlightenment about the eternal rules of the Dao.[54] [Comprehending] the eternal rules of the Dao and going through the ten thousand mutations – this is to firmly give foundations and roots to one's inner nature. The highest inner nature will penetrate the ultimate,[55] no material substance [will undergo] the ten thousand mutations, and the ten thousand spontaneous communications are like the supreme wisdom. The square is rounded, the crooked is straightened - the ten thousand schools will be pure. One will communicate with all streams[56] and enter the Great Oceans. And thus, that which originated in the primordial chaos will return into the One. This is called "the deep communication."

The inner nature of man may be clever or dull; by those [properties the inner nature] may lie in concealment. (DZ 122.5b-6a)

As for the interior of of the men of antiquity who realized the Dao, [their] inner nature was wise and clever, [their actions] were appropriate, and they had compassion. If the exterior of man is evil or dull, [then] by those [properties the inner nature] may lie in concealment; the interior light may be hidden and not apparent. *Heshang gong*

---

54 Chin. *daochang* 道常. In DZ 1058, 13a –14b, Liu Chuxuan comments on the word 'chang,' here translated as 'eternal rules': "The eternal rules – that is the Dao. When one is constantly (*chang*) in accordance with one's Dao, he saves the human soul. When one is constantly in accordance with the *qi*, he saves the physical form. When man is constanly in accordance with the Dao, he is like a fish in water."

55 Chin. *Taij* 太及.

56 Lit. "the *Chang Jiang, the Huang He, the River Huai and the River Ji,"* Chin. *jianghehuaiji* 江河淮濟. These are the four great rivers of China and they represent all streams of the civilized world. Here, however, they serve a metaphorical purpose, standing for the bodily fluids.

says: "Beautiful jade dwelling in the stone resembles the brilliant pearl in the oyster."[57] Among the birds, it is the uncommonly clever oriole, which is capable of words. [But] the voice of the dull dove imprisoned in an iron cage resounds in the ten thousand leaves all over.[58]

For this reason, the worldly men are false and clever, and thus they bring forth ten thousand calamities.[59] Perfect dullness arises from purity and good fortune.[60] Therefore, Heaven does not speak,[61] and naturally it is thoroughly transformed. Heaven has no sentiments, and naturally it does not age. When man is enlightened about the Dao of Heaven and forgets speech, then he will discover the subtlety of the creational process. He forgets the sentiments, and thus he will be enlightened and revert to the demeanor of antiquity. As for all the human desires: If there is too much cleverness, there will also be many transgressions. If there are too many sentiments, there will also be much suffering. If one forgets the world and abandons the sentiments, then he will enjoy the Dao and he will guard the requirements of existence.

---

57 Here, Liu Chuxuan quotes the famous first commentary on the *Daodejing*, the *Laozi daodejing heshang gong zhangju* 老子道德經河上公章句 which was one of the two commentaries on classical scriptures that Ma Danyang recommended for followers of *Quanzhen* in DZ 1057, 10a. However, Liu Chuxuan's quote is not very accurate. Commenting on the opening sentence of the *Daodejing* "The Name which becomes the Name is not the eternal Name," the *Heshang gong* has: "As to the eternal Dao, it is like the baby-child who does not speak yet, it is like the fowls which do not separate [things] yet, and [as] the brilliant pearl is in the oyster, and beautiful jade dwells in the stone, it is shining on the inside, but ignorant and stupid on the outside." (The translation is my own, for the Chinese source see DZ 682 *Daode zhenjing zhu* 1.1a or for a modern edition Wang Ka, *Laozi daodejing heshang gong zhangju*, Beijing: Zhonghua shuju, 1993, p.1.)

58 Lit. "horizontally and vertically," Chin. *zongheng* 縱橫.

59 Lit. "ten thousand calamities," Chin. *wanhuo* 萬禍.

60 Although the grammatical structure of this sentence seems more than obvious, the strong parallelism developed in this passage may indicate that the word *yu* (in, at, from) was added to the original source. Thus, we would have: "For this reason, my contemporaries are false and clever, and thus they bring forth ten thousand calamities. Perfect dullness brings forth purity and good fortune."

61 In DZ 1058, 31b, Liu Chuxuan refers to Heaven's silent acting when explaining the word 'practice' (Chin. *xing* 行): "As for the word 'practice' – the practice of the Highest [Lord Lao] is the Dao of Heaven. Heaven and Earth do not speak, yet they secretely exercise their mercy and bring forth among the ten thousand beings. The Highest [Lord Lao] does not speak, yet he secretly practices his virtue among the ten thousand beings. Heaven and Earth do not speak, and mercy and the good are in accordance."

The disruption of the nine orifices[62] lies in the three principles; by them one may be active or quiescent. (DZ 122.6a-b)

The nine orifices are the Yang roads of the nine communications.[63] When they do not yet communicate, they are the gates to the depravity of the nine Yin. The human mind is a square-inch,[64] in its void there is a numinous brightness. The minds of the highest men have nine orifices. The men in the middle have seven orifices, and the lowest men have five orifices. If the mind has no orifices, one speaks of foolish men. The depraved Yin is born, and the inner nature becomes corrupted; the light of the Yang ascends, and the spirits become pure.

[It] lies in the three principles:
The radiance of Heaven has the sun, the moon and the stars. The treasures of Earth have gold, jade and gems. The entire Dao has lead, mercury and perfection.[65]

By them one may be active or quiescent:
When Heaven is active, the three beams are illuminating. When Earth is quiescent, the three treasures communicate. When the subtle is shining, the three mysteries congeal. As for activity, activity lies in the physical form. As for quiescence, quiescence lies in the inner nature. The sages of antiquity lived hidden in a disordered world, yet their minds were inactive. They lived on the mountains, yet they did not display quiescence in their physical form. If one understands being, being is quiescent in activity; if one communicates with the non-being, the non-being does not re-

---

62 Traditionally, the *nine orifices*, Chin. *jiuqiao* 九竅, are the nine openings of the body. Here, however, the *Yinfu jing* and Liu Chuxuan's commentary understand the *nine orifices* as referring to the mind and thus as a spiritual entity.

63 Chin. *tong* 通 is a central term throughout Liu Chuxuan's commentary. It is not easily translated. Sometimes, I translate it as "penetrate" or "penetration", sometimes, as in this case, "communication" seems more appropriate. Here, *tong* refers to a state of being when the nine orifices open up to the beneficial influences of *Yang*.

64 The expression "square-inch," Chin. *fangcun* 方寸, can refer to the human mind or heart itself, but also to one of the three "cinnabar fields" in the human body. In the scripture *Huangting waijie jing*, one of the central scriptures of *Shangqing*-Daoism and also one of the main sources of reference for the authors of inner alchemy texts, we find that *fangcun* refers to the *yellow court*. The *yellow court* is the lower cinnabar field and also the point in the body where the meditating subject must direct his mental energies. For a translation and an explanation of the three cinnabar fields see Michael Saso, *The Gold Pavilion: Taoist ways to peace, healing, and long life*, Rutland, Vermont and Tokyo: Charles E. Tuttle Co., Inc., 1995, p. 106-7.

65 In DZ 121, 8b, Tang Chun comments on the same passage: "As for the three principles, they are the ears, the eyes and the mouth."

sound in quiescence. Forget both activity and quiescence, and thus you will attain the eternal magical mystery of the Dao.[66]

When the element fire originates in wood, calamities will break out, and the wood will surely succumb.
When treachery originates in a state, time will be disturbed,
and the state will surely collapse. One who knows this and cultivates [his consciousness of it] is called a sage. (DZ 122.6b-7b)

Fire gives birth to the human mind. It happens daily and everywhere. The unchanging[67] evil lies in wood, and thus it becomes the inner nature of man. If one's thoughts are not enlightened, the fire ignites the inner nature, which is [made of the element] wood.[68]

Calamities will break out, and the wood will surely succumb:
When auspicious signs are disregarded, bad omens [arise]; when good fortune is destroyed, calamities will come. The word "succumb" means that [under these circumstances] one kills the truth.

Treachery originates in a state:
The Scripture of the Highest[69] says: "He who does not rule the state by his knowledge is a blessing for the state. He who rules the state by his knowledge is a thief to the country."[70] When flattery and deceitful people are born in the state, it is that the ten thousand people will hardly be without difficulties. Time will be disturbed, and

---

66 Chin. *dao zhi changmiao* 道之常妙.
67 Lit. "that which does not change ten thousand times," Chin. *buwanbian zhi* 不萬變之.
68 Here, Liu Chuxuan's commentary remains extremely cryptic. In Tang Chun's commentary on the *Yinfu jing* that I have referred to occasionally before we find the following explanation of this passage: "As for [the expression] 'fire gives birth to wood,' the Dao of Heaven means walking against the normal course of nature. When wood gives birth to fire, this is the Dao if Earth and walking according to the normal course of nature." (See DZ 121, 9b.)
69 "The Highest," Chin. *taishang* 太上, is an abbreviation for "The highest Lord Lao," Chin. *taishang laojun* 太上老君, the name of the deified Laozi. Thus, the "scripture of the Highest" is the *Daode jing* whose author was Laozi.
70 See the 65th chapter of the *Dade jing*, DZ 664, 18b.

the state will surely collapse and disperse.[71] The foolish have no principles, and they [cause] turmoil in the state. And one must meet this with punishments. He who does not rule the state by his knowledge will rule the world with no problems. [And thus] the world and the people will be in Great Peace.[72] He who knows this does not cultivate and practice the cultivation and practice of heating the nine [kinds of] metals and the eight [kinds of] stones.

If one cultivates [both] inner nature and existence,[73] he will attain the ideal and communicate with the mysteries. The three teachings call this "realizing the Dao." Always saving the creatures, having compassion for the world and knowing the mercy of heaven – this is called "accumulating virtue." Due to the Yellow Emperor's realization of the Dao there is this *Scripture of the Hidden Contracts*. In the times of the Zhou dynasty, king Jinlun was awakened to Buddhism, and thus there is this Diamond Sutra. After he had turned into the Buddha his name became Shakyamuni Buddha.[74] The thirty-two chapters of *The Diamond Sutra* speak of the essentials of his teachings.[75] One should abandon the external perception of the ego, the perception of man,[76] the perception of all living beings and the perception of longevity. If those four perceptions[77] no longer exist, there will be none of the ten thousand faults in the human mind at all. Like a Heaven without clouds, the inner nature will resemble the shining moon. Self-evident and shining radiantly, this is the true inner nature.

---

71 Here, Liu Chuxuan uses the wording of the *Yinfu jing* and adds one word of his own, the verb "disperse". The assumption that the text might omit the grammatical particle *zhe* after the quote from the *Yinfujing* would make an alternative reading possible here: "The sentence 'Time will be disturbed, and the state will surely collapse' means dispersion."
72 Chin. *taiping min'an* 太平民安, lit. "Great peace and pacified people."
73 The concepts of the simultaneous cultivation of inner nature and physical existence, Chin. *xingming shuangxiu* 性命雙修, is certainly one of the main topics in Liu Chuxuan's commentary. It is also one of the defining features of *Quanzhen*-Daoism. It can be found in a variety of scriptures in the *Daozang* authored by the founder of the *Quanzhen*-school, Wang Zhe and his foremost disciples. For my discussion of this term and Liu Chuxuan's position on the issue, see the fourth chapter of this study.
74 Chin. *shijiamonifo* 釋迦牟尼佛.
75 Chin. *dao* 道.
76 E.g., the perception that man is a being different from other beings. See Soothill, p.179.
77 The four perceptions mentioned here go back to the *Diamond Sutra*. In its third chapter, the Buddha says: "And why not, Subhuti? A bodhisattva who has the perception of a an ego, the perception of man, the perception of all living beings and the perception of longevity cannot be a bodhisattva." See *T*. 235.2.

The inner nature is like the roots of a tree. The body is like the human form. The ten thousand methods are like the branches and the leaves of a tree. The guidance to the creational process of the *Scripture of the Hidden Contracts* is like blooming flowers and like sprouting seeds.

When the worldly men study the Dao it is said that they cannot completely penetrate its principles. Falsely, they still hold to all distinctions and differences, and they still hold to the roots and leafs, the blossoms and the sprouting seeds. And therefore, they are wronged, and their minds have not yet abandoned the four distinctions. This is called the minor schools.

The middle chapter: Enriching the state and pacifying the people: On civil law.

Heaven gives life and Heaven gives death – such is the principle of the Dao. Heaven and Earth are thieves of the ten thousand creatures; the ten thousand creatures are thieves of man; and man is a thief of the ten thousand creatures. In this way, the three thieves are all in accord, and the three cosmic elements[78] are all at peace. (DZ 122.8a-b)

Heaven gives life and Heaven gives death:
When the harmonious *qi* [arise from] the warmth of spring, Heaven gives birth among the ten thousand creatures. But when fall arrives and deepens, the west-wind[79] is activated, [and thus] the ten thousand creatures rotten and cripple. This is when Heaven gives death. Giving birth and giving death is the principle of the Dao. Heaven has no sentiments but it is spontaneous.

Heaven and Earth are thieves of the ten thousand creatures:
As for Heaven and Earth, the transformations of the four seasons adjust to the creational process; and they bear and complete the ten thousand creatures. All the flourishing *qi* of Heaven and Earth, of Yin and of Yang hidden in the ten thousand creatures are the flourishing *qi* stolen [from Heaven and Earth] by the ten thousand creatures.

---

78 Chin. *sancai*三才. The "three cosmic elements" are Heaven, Earth and Man. See the third chapter of this study.
79 Lit. "*metal-wind*," Chin. *jinfeng*金風. According to traditional Chinese thought, the element metal is associated with the west and with fall.

The ten thousand creatures are thieves of man:
All the essences of the ten thousand creatures stolen by man are the flourishing *qi* taken away from Heaven and Earth. Destroy desires, have your thoughts be pure and quiescent – this is to maintain and to guard existence.

Man is a thief of the ten thousand creatures:
As for the splendid spheres of the ten thousand creatures[80] that man desires, the eyes see the five colors, the ears hear the five tones, and the tongue tastes the five flavors.[81] Drink and feast – and you will be foul and slovenly! Follow the false and engage in lewd actions – and the existence will be destroyed! Thus the ultimate joy is grievance. If man renounces the world and is enlightened, there will be no sentiments, and thus there will be nothing the external things could steal from man.

The three thieves are all in accord:
All theft is infinite, the highest treasures and the creational process complete the physical form. One can hardly haggle over the price of the world's ten thousand *hu*[82] of precious things.[83]

The three cosmic forces are all at peace:
Revert in accordance with the three holy teachings[84] and illuminate the three vehicles; understand the mysteries of the three emperors[85]; let the three luminaries[86] circulate above, overthrow the three vehicles, plow and reveal the three fields,[87] and the

---

80　Chin. *wanwu zhi huajing* 萬物之華景.
81　The five colors, the five tones and the five flavors are believed to be the primary source of distraction from the cultivation of the Dao. And thus, they stand for the entire world of sensation. In the twelfth chapter of the *Daodejing,* we find: "The five colors make our eyes blind/ the five tones make our ears deaf/ the five flavors make our mouths numb/ riding and hunting make our minds wild." See DZ 664 *Daode zhenjing*, 3b.
82　A *hu* is an ancient Chinese measurement, holding ten pecks before the southern song period and five afterwards. See *Ciyuan*, Beijing 1998, p. 741.
83　This is not entirely clear. I assume that the 'precious things' Liu Chuxuan refers to here are the aforementioned 'highest treasures' of religious Daoism that are opposed to the material goods that worldly men value.
84　Chin. *sanshengjiao* 三聖教. The three holy teachings are Daoism, Confucianism and Buddhism.
85　The three sacred emperors of China's legendary past: *Fuxi*, the divine farmer *Shennong* and the yellow emperor *Huangdi*.
86　The "three luminaries," Chin. *sanguang* 三光, are the sun, the moon and the stars. See *Ciyuan*, p.16a.
87　The "three fields" are probably the three cinnabar fields described in the *Huangting neijie jing* (*The Inner Scripture of the Yellow Court*). The cinnabar fields are the three spaces in

three fire-furnaces of the orbiting Heaven will let the three elixirs congeal, the spirits will reveal the three Yang and rise up to the three Heavens. One will be perfected, but not decay; one will live, but not perish. The exhaustion of the material substance– this is the Dao. When both perfection and the Dao form the same body, then it will be peace.

Therefore it is said, "Eat at the proper time, and the body will be properly ordered; activated at their points of actuation, the ten thousand transformations will be in peace." Men know their spirits as spirits, but they do not know why the non-spirited is a spirit. (DZ 122.8b-10a)

Eat at the proper time:
When one encounters wonderful delicacies in times of starvation, he does not desire those, and when one finds coarse foods [in times of starvation], he does not reject those; one does not kill living beings or eat rotten foods, nor cultivate fasting or eat vegetarian foods. In times of starvation, no matter if [the food is] coarse or fine, when one feels tired, he sleeps; when one feels leisurely, he sings; when one feels happy, he hums. When one wants to meditate, he meditates;[88] when one wants to lie down, he lies down; when one wants to pause, he pauses; when one wants to walk, he walks. If one relinquishes the Great Four[89] and does not adhere to one's own exis-

---

the human body where the mind of the Daoist has to be focused during meditation or other practices of inner alchemy.

88 Lit. "sit," Chin. *zuo* 坐.
89 Lit. "the four great," Chin. *sida* 四大. The concept of the "great four" has two different origins. In the *Daode jing* it refers to the four greatest beings of the cosmos: the Dao, Heaven, Earth and Man. However, in Buddhism the term refers to the concept that every being is composed of four basic substances: earth, water, fire and wind. Later Daoism borrowed this concept from Buddhism. (See ZHDJDCD, Zhonghua shudian, Beijing 1995, p.453.) Wang Chongyang, the founder of the *Quanzhen*-school, writes in his scripture DZ 1158, 3a –3b, *Chongyang zhenren shou danyang zhenren ershisi jue* 重陽真人授丹陽二十四訣 (Fourteen Secret Methods Wang Chongyang bestowed to Ma Danyang): "Heaven has four seasons, man has the great four. Heaven has earth, water, fire and wind; man has the mind, the essences, the *qi* and the body. [...] And as for Heaven having earth, water, fire and wind, these are metal, wood, water, fire and earth. And as for man having earth, water, fire and wind, the mind is fire, the essence is water, the *qi* are wind and the body is earth. And thus [man] is earth, water, fire and wind." Liu Chuxuan's commentary clearly refers to the Buddhist concept as explained in Wang Chongyang's writings. The fact that

tence, the body[90] will be ideally ordered. In respect to the ten thousand shadows during the twelve hours, the true mind must only always be pristine.[91]
But as for activity, activity cannot arise from the mind. Internally, the echoes and the radiance of the treasures appear. The material substance is active in the physical form.

As for trigger:
The saints, the sages and the gentlemen call it "wisdom," the generals call it "stratagem," the common men call it "trigger," the vulgar men call it "escape to the void." The saints are great in wisdom and deep in principles. The wordly men cannot completely[92] understand their principles. [The saints] cherished the subtle knowledge, and [their] mouth was in accord with the eternal trigger. Those who are faithful listen, and those who are wise follow. When the ten thousand complete explications cause sudden enlightenment then there will be peace and tranquility, and the Dao will rise.[93]

Men know the spirits as spirits:
The worldly men only know the earthly gods and the Yin-spirits as spirits. Spirits carved in wood and formed from mud are treated as [true] spirits. The foolish do not know that Heaven will send down calamities and sorrows that befit every mistake they make. They kill and harm pigs and lambs, they burn [paper-] money and [paper-] horses, and they pray. When they are sick, they search for peace. When they encounter calamities, they search for good luck.[94]

---

the founder of *Quanzhen-Daoism*, Wang Chongyang, employs the same concept in his own writings may indicate the influence he had on Liu Chuxuan's thought.
90 Lit. "the one hundred bones," Chin. *baihai*百骸.
91 Liu Chuxuan expresses a similar notion concerning the practitioner's demanded indifference towards food and eating in the collection of sayings of early Quanzhen masters DZ1256 *Zhenxian zhizhi yulu*真仙直指語錄, 1.10a, where he is quoted with the following words:"The highest Lord says those who can beg and eat are my brothers and sons. There is profit in begging."
92 Lit. "exhaustive," Chin. *jin*盡.
93 Lit. "Dao will be born," Chin. *dao sheng*道生.
94 Here, the commentary refers to superstitious religious practices. Liu Chuxuan condemns these practices as inconsistent with the Dao of Heaven. In this passage, the revolutionary tendency of *Quanzhen* becomes most obvious. From his point of view, *Quanzhen* was not only one religious movement among others; it marked a departure from a spiritually corrupted world that had become incapable of a true relationship with the Dao of Heaven.

But they do not know why the non-spirited is a spirit:

[The worldly men] do not know the Dao of the supreme Yang of Heaven. The highest spirits secretly examine every location for the good and the evil in the human realm. When the wordly men perform good [deeds] three years but no more than a thousand days, [Heaven] sends down auspicious signs and good omens. But when men perform evil [deeds] a thousand days but no more than three years, Heaven sends down calamities and sorrows.

The wordly men do not know that [their own] self is the mightiest and most sensible being among the ten thousand creatures. The primordial spirits posses a light penetrating Heaven and Earth. The sages and saints of antiquity completely realized this Dao and cultivated perfection. They emerged from the common [world] and entered sagacity. In the western paradise, a Buddha reached a life of twenty-eight generations. When the Buddha has not yet practiced cultivation, he is still like all creatures. But when he has brought purity and quiescence to the six roots,[95] when his five eyes are radiantly shining, and when he has destroyed the four perceptions, his name becomes that of a Buddha.

The Buddha is the inner nature of man. "Inner nature" means the spirit. The inner nature, this is the spirit. The spirit, this is the inner nature. They are only different names. As for Buddhism, when the inner nature has abandoned the four perceptions, one speaks of a "Buddha". As for Daoism, when the spirit forgets about the four perceptions, one speaks of an immortal.

The sun and the moon have periodicities, and the small and the large have delimitations. Sagacity and merits emerge from there and [those who are] spiritual and enlightened emerge from them. (DZ 122.10a-11a)

The sun and the moon have periodicities:
When the sixty *ke*[96] of the summer solstice decrease gradually, the one Yin is born. And when the 40 *ke* of the winter solstice accumulate gradually, the one Yang is born. In the period between five and seven in the morning the sun rises above the Eastern Sea. In the period between five and seven in the evening the sun sets in the

---

95 Chin. *liugen qingjing* 六根清淨. This Buddhist concept refers to the purification of the six organs in order to achieve the fullest enlightenment. When this state of being is attained, the respective person is able to see everything in the entire cosmos, for instance the karma of every being. See W. E. Soothill, p.135b.

96 Chin. *ke* 刻 is an ancient Chinese time-unit. Day and night are divided into one hundred *ke*. The summer day has sixty-five *ke*, whereas the winter day has no more than forty-five *ke*.

Western Mountains. The Scripture of Purity and Tranquility[97] says: "The Great Dao has no sentiments. It [just] lets sun and moon revolve [in their orbits]."[98] As to the sun, the luminance of wisdom[99] revolves, draws and supplements.[100]

[They] have periodicities:
As to the moon,[101] man's fate lies in [its having periodicities]. At the age of sixteen, the adolescent boy completes his true [element] metal of two-eight.[102] If he does not realize [the concept of] no sentiments, he will lose one liang in three years and reach eight times eight. The sixty-four hexagrams[103] will be exhausted and thus the kidney-sea will be dried up. If one has too many desires, then an early death occurs even before the hexagrams have been exhausted. If one reduces the desires, he gains longevity and an extended duration of life. When waxing and waning [like the moon], man dies. When completed [rounded-up] and never diminishing, man lives.[104]

---

97 Chin. *qingjing jing* 清靜經.
98 The quote is accurate. It stems from the text DZ 620, 1a, *Qingjing miaojing* 清靜妙經 (*Subtle Scripture of Purity and Tranquility*). This text, probably written in the 9th century, is one of the most prominent sources for the *Quanzhen*-school. See Livia Kohn and Russel Kirkland, *Daoism in the Tang*, in: Livia Kohn (ed.), Daoism Handbook, p.363. The importance of this text is also reflected in the fact that its title became part of the Daoist name of honor for Liu Chuxuan: *Changsheng qingjing wuwei zhenren*.
99 Chin. *huiguang* 慧光. This term is borrowed from Buddhist thought. However, in Buddhism it generally refers to the interior light of wisdom brighter than the light of sun and moon.
100 Chin. *choutian* 抽添.
101 Lit. "the moon which has periodicities."
102 The term "two-eight" (Chin. *erba* 二八) refers to a concept that belongs to the traditions of *inner alchemy*. It symbolizes the equilibrium of the two energetic emblems *Yin* and *Yang* and a state of perfect harmony of the five elements. See ZHDJDCD, p.1190.
103 Chin. *liushisi gua* 六十四卦, the sixty-four complex diagrams from the *Yi Jing* 易經, the Classic of Changes. Obviously, in this part of his commentary Liu Chuxuan draws heavily on the Chinese numerology and cosmology based on the *Yi jing*.
104 This passage elucidates Liu Chuxuan's knowledge of the theory of *inner alchemy*. By using the soteriological language derived from the *Yijing*, Liu Chuxuan explains the relationship between the macrocosmic and microcosmic processes in the human body that lead to decay and death. In the last passage of his commentary, Liu Chuxuan explains how one can reverse this inevitable process and restore the primordial energies. See the first chapter of this study.

Small and large have delimitations:
The large is the Dao. The greatness of the Dao contains Heaven and Earth. The small is the invisible. The discussion of the invisible enters the smallest particles. It circulates, but Heaven and Earth cannot measure it. It functions, but the ghosts and the spirits cannot perceive it. The delimitation of spontaneity resides in the square-inch.[105]

Sagacity and merits emerge from there:
This is the Dao of Heaven. When the great mercy of Heaven arises, it aids man in nourishing his physical form. When the sagacity and the merits of the Dao emerge, they aid man in the cultivation of perfection.

The spirit and enlightenment arise from there:
Hidden the spirit roams in the three palaces; perceptible the spirit communicates with the eight cardinal points.[106]

The thievery – that is the trigger. In the entire world,[107] there is no one who can see it and there is nobody who can know it. If a wise man seizes it, he will be confirmed in his poverty. If a vulgar man seizes it, he will [only] make light of life. (DZ 122.11a-b)

The trigger of thievery:
It is the trigger of the ten thousand creatures that steals the *qi* from Heaven and Earth.
In the entire world, there is nobody who can see it:
Heaven's great mercy gives birth [to the ten thousand creatures].

[In the entire world,] there is nobody who can know it:
The foolish only know how to nourish their body. They do not know that Heaven sends down mercy and nourishes the ten thousand people. Spring sows, fall harvests, summer blooms, and winter stores. In accordance with the seasons, frost and snow, rain and dew let the ten thousand transformations sprout and flourish. As for those

---

105 Lit. "square-inch," Chin. *fangcun*方寸; an alternative expression used for the human heart or mind, Chin. *xin*心. In the *Huangting neijie jing*, the expression "square/inch" is also used for the gold pavilion, the central focus of energy in the human body.
106 Chin. *babiao*八表. The eight *cardinal points* refer to the space outside the eight directions north, east, south, west, northeast, southeast, southwest and northwest. As such, they represent areas far out of reach of the normal consciousness. See *Ciyuan*, Beijing 1998, p.161.
107 Lit. "That which is under Heaven," Chin. *tianxia*天下.

among the worldly men who know about the mercy of Heaven, their inner nature communicates [with the Dao], and they have attained enlightenment.

If the gentleman seizes it, he will be confirmed in his poverty:
Poverty communicates with the Dao, and thus Heaven and Earth communicate. Heaven and Earth communicate, and thus the ten thousand transformations communicate. The ten thousand transformations communicate, and thus the spirits communicate. The spirits communicate, and thus the ten thousand transformations are in accordance with the trigger, and they embrace the One;[108] and in solitude, one nurtures perfection and returns to the spiritual substance.[109]

If a vulgar man seizes it he will only make light of life:
If a vulgar man seizes it, he will insult and deceive Heaven and Earth; he will not praise virtue and sagacity; he will not respect the laws of the country; he will not have humanity and he will not be righteous[110]; he will let himself be strong and let the others weaken; he will hurt both the creatures and mankind. [He commits] the most extreme faults, and thus Heaven will retaliate. The great inner nature of the gentleman attains communication with virtue and sagacity; the light existence of the vulgar man causes him to lose [his life], and [he] falls to be reborn as an animal.[111]

---

108 The One represents the eternal Dao that is found in every human being.
109 Chin. *pu* 朴, literally 'uncarved wood.'
110 Chin. *ren* 仁, and *yi* 義, both Confucian virtues.
111 Literally the commentary speaks of "the heavy inner nature of the gentleman," Chin. *junzi zhongxing* 君子重性, and "the light physical existence of the vulgar man," Chin. *xiaoren qingming* 小人輕命. The *Yinfu jing* itself contains only the latter expression. Obviously, Liu Chuxuan wants to make his point by using those antithetical expressions. Generally, Liu Chuxuan's commentary seems to favor the simultaneous cultivation of both *xing* and *ming*. But in this passage the two terms are used to demonstrate the difference between sagacity and vulgarity. While the vulgar man aspires to lightness in his physical existence, the inner nature of the sagacious man is heavy.

The lower chapter: Strengthening soldiers for victories in battles: On [military] methods.

The blind are skilled in listening; the deaf are skilled in observing Cut off the one source of profits, the employment of one's forces will be successful ten times over. By reverting day and night three times, the employment of one's forces will be [successful] ten times over. (DZ 122.11b-12b)

The blind are skilled in listening:
The eyes of man are the windows to the five viscera.[112] If one communicates with the wind, he will gaze at the exterior things. Just as paper-screens and remote winds are separated from each other, the blind cannot see the exterior things. If the exterior appearances do not enter the center, the true echoes arise from the void, and one will be skilled in listening to the sound of the soundless.[113]

The deaf are skilled in observing:
And when the vulgar *qi* of the world arrives at the ears, then one is like the deaf. When the thoughts of the Dao[114] arrive at the ears, then one hears. Those who speak in a depraved manner are also like the deaf. And as for the virtuous who choose the correct and the principles, the orifices of their ears communicate; and this occurs as the knocking down of the walls lets the exterior light come inside. They observe the immaterial things and then they understand the obscure mysteries.

Cut off the one source of profits:
Forget greed, and there will be purity and peace. And also, when profits are destroyed and goods are horded, excessive losses will occur and kindness will be insufficient. One who lives in the utmost solitude and enlightenment is rewarded ten times over. One who benefits creatures and loves mankind earns good fortune ten times over.

By reverting day and night three times:

---

[112] Chin. *wuzang*五臟. The five viscera are the liver, the kidneys, the lungs, the heart and the spleen. This term refers to the complete physical existence of man, i.e. the whole body.
[113] Lit. "sound without sound," Chin. *wusheng zhi sheng*無聲之聲.
[114] Chin. *daonian*道念.

First, reverting the Upper Prime grants good fortune, *qi* will descend, and thus there will be purity. Second, reverting the Middle Prime remits the sins, and the spirits will be uncommonly mighty. Third, reverting the Lower Prime dissolves distress, the existence will communicate, and thus Yin will turn into Yang.[115]

The employment of one's forces will be [successful] ten times over:
The wordly men focus on trading material goods. Those who gain a larger profit hardly gain a profit one time over. He who realizes Dao and cultivates perfection completes [both] his inner nature and existence, gaining inexhaustible good fortune and long life. Living in the immortal's palaces, treasuring the heavenly wealth and ranks one receives, compared to the fortunes and profits that man strives for, is ten thousand times more valuable. The sea turning into mulberry orchards, eternally dwelling in the land without nights – how could this perfect joy accrue to a profit only ten times over?

The mind is born in [the context of] matter, and it dies in [the context of] matter. The point of actuation lies in the eyes. (DZ 122.12b-13a)

The mind is born in [the context of] matter, but it belongs [to the realm] outside of matter.

It dies in:
When the mind dies, it will communicate with the spirited beings.[116] When the worldly men pursue [the way of] life, the inner nature will return on the road of death. When one attains Dao [on the other hand], he will respect death, and the spirits will travel on the road of life. The Dao and the vulgar [way] and life and death are different roads, and they are mutually exclusive.

The point of actuation lies in the eyes:
The eyes see in [the context of] matter, [but] the mind is activated by the trigger. When there is profit, there is also harm. When there is greed, there is also struggle. When the eye of intelligence[117] sees the spiritual beings, when it is enlightened about the trigger of Heaven and knows the deep mystery of the Dao, [the distinctions] of things and of the ego will all be destroyed.

---

115 In inner alchemy, the term 'the three primes,' Chin. *sanyuan* 三元, refers to the three cinnabar fields. Since the three cinnabar fields are each identified with one of the 'three treasures,' the three primes can also refer to essence, *qi* and spirit. See ZHDJDC, p.1140.
116 Chin. *lingwu* 靈物.
117 Chin. *huimu* 慧目.

The vulgar trigger benefits the self, but injures mankind. The trigger of the Dao injures the self, but benefits mankind.

Heaven has no mercy, but great mercy arises from it. It causes swift thunder and violent winds, and there is no one who does not come from simplicity.[118] (DZ 122.13a-b)

Heaven has no mercy:
By distributing *qi*, [Heaven] gives birth to matter, yet it does not posses [anything].[119]

And yet great mercy arises from it:
The ten thousand creatures are born and completed [by Heaven]. If the ten thousand creatures did not obtain the *qi* of Heaven and Earth, they would not be able to [enter] the creational process and complete the physical form. As for Heaven, great mercy arises from it; if it does not have mercy, it is [because] Heaven does not expect any compensation.

As for man's mercy, when I see someone who has it, he expects compensation. Heaven's mercy and man's mercy are different. When swift thunder resounds,[120] sweet rain will drop from Heaven. When Earth brings forth violent winds, clouds will float up and disperse over ten thousand miles, and Heaven will be blue.

There are none who do not come from simplicity:[121]
Simplicity is active and dwells in the four classes of birth.[122] There is no one who does not receive the one *qi* of Heaven. And how is it then that a being without sentiments is born among the ten thousand beings?

---

118 Here, Christopher C. Rand's translation is certainly closer to the *Yinfu jing* than mine. Rand's translation has: "Heaven's lack of mercy is yet great mercy. [It engenders] swift thunder and violent winds, and there are none who are not dumb-founded." However, Liu Chuxuan's reading of the *Yinfu jing* does not justify this translation.
119 Chin. *buqi sheng wu er buyou* 布氣生物而不有. This passage recalls a sentence in the *Daodejing*, chapter 51: "It gives birth but yet it does not posses (Chin. *sheng er buyou* 生而不有)."
120 Lit. "cry (like a bird)," Chin. *ming* 鳴.
121 Chin. *chunran* 蠢然. Christopher Rand's translation has 'dumb-founded'; however literally, this term refers to an unspoiled state of being. Liu Chuxuan's commentary supports my translation, since he associates this sentence with the 'four classes of birth.'
122 Chin. *tailuanshihua* 胎卵濕化. This term, literally 'the womb, the egg, moist and metamorphosis," signifies the origins of all beings in Buddhist thought. The four terms appear in the *Diamond Sutra* where they represent deluding perceptions and distinctions: "How-

In ultimate happiness the inner nature is unlimited; in ultimate quiescence the inner nature is uncorrupted. (DZ 122.13b-14a)

He who finds eternal joy in the inner nature of the Dao is unlimited. He who finds satisfaction in the body and the world is constrained. I do not feel pleasure, and thus I do not feel grief. When man has joy, he has sadness, too. Realize the true rules of undisturbed tranquility, the deceitful sounds and colors and the erroneous worldly dreams!

In ultimate quiescence the inner nature is uncorrupted:
When ultimate quiescence is [achieved], then it exhausts matter. The inner nature being uncorrupted, this is like the lotus, which does not belong to the water. Those men who have attained the Dao live amidst the [world of] dust, yet they are not contaminated [by it]. As far as desires are concerned, they do not have them. Polished, the mirror of the treasures reflects the shadows of the material form. Not even one class of obstacles enters the center. As for those who have realized the Dao, they recognize the ultimate quiescence in the faintest light. They abandon being and dwell in non-being. They relinquish the illusory thoughts of being, the distinctions in low and high [things], and they broaden the magic power of virtue and Dao.

The worldly men are like hemp.[123] According to the Highest's *Daode jing*, it is said: "The virtuous speech is not beautiful, the beautiful speech is not virtuous. The true speech of the correct Dao is not beautiful." The depraved method is falsely transmitted and very beautiful. Those who care for [this speech], will clearly love its beauty. Because of this they belong to [the realm] of the depraved and cannot attain the Great Dao.

The ultimate partiality of Heaven is ultimate impartiality in its applications. (DZ 122.14a-b)

Heaven practices mercy, but it does not let those below [Heaven] know about it. And this is [Heaven's] partiality. Heaven bears and completes [the ten thousand creatures], and it aids the human world.[124] And this is [Heaven's] ultimate impartiality.

---

ever many classes of living beings there are, whether they were born from an egg, from the womb, from moist or from metamorphosis, whether they have form or no form, whether they have thought or no thought or neither thought nor no thought, in whatever realm of being one could conceive of beings, I will let them enter the nirvana and liberate them all." See *T.* 235.1.

123 Chin. *ma* 麻, also "numbed" or "drugged".
124 Heaven's secret mercy is a topic in DZ 1058, 31b.

When a man has the Dao, it is like Jade hidden in a stone. The physical eye[125] of the worldly men cannot yet see this gem. When it is sharpened and polished, and completely finished another day, the body outside the body will appear.

The raw substance is distributed and forms great vessels. Those men who do not have the Dao resemble wood full of worms. The eyes of Heaven have a gaze like the sun. Use the axe and the saw and cut off the rotten and the ragged, and immediately the *hun*-soul will fly, the *po*-soul will be dispersed. If the inner nature is corrupted, one sinks eternally into hell. If one cultivates the Dao and has compassion for all creatures, bitterness will be exhausted and sweetness will arrive. Create evil and ask for good fortune – the ten thousand calamities will come close to the body. Those who follow the will of Heaven go against [the usual course of nature]; those who act against the will of Heaven follow [the usual course of nature].[126] When the gentleman achieves the utmost wisdom, he pays reverence to the Dao and its virtue. Heaven's compensation seems to be ultimate partiality, but it is wholly ultimate impartiality. When the vulgar man participates in the low and ordinary man's competition for sensuality and wealth, Heaven's compensation is ultimate impartiality at first, but eventually it is ultimate partiality.[127]

---

125 Lit. "the eye of flesh," Chin. *rouyan*肉眼. The "eye of flesh" is a Buddhist term. See Soothill, p.219. In DZ 1058, 5a, Liu Chuxuan explains the term "seeing": "Seeing, this does not refer to anything the eyes of flesh can see. Seeing, this refers to seeing one's void and non-being."

126 Chin. *tianyi shunzhe nixing nizhe shunxing* 天意順者逆行逆者順行. In this passage, Liu Chuxuan plays a word game with the two terms *ni* 逆 and *shun* 順. In inner alchemy, it is assumed that processes in ordinary life follow the course of nature, and as a result, those who are in accord with those processes die. The goal of inner alchemy is to revert the ordinary course of nature, i.e. the normal productive order of the five elements. The person who succeeds in doing so gains immortality. For a concise discussion of the two terms and the concepts involved, see the first chapter of this study. See also Joseph Needham and Lu Gwei-Djen, *Science and Civilisation in China. Vol. 5, Part V*, Taibei, 1986 (reprint), p.59. In DZ 1058, 3b, Liu Chuxuan gives the following explanations of the word 'knowledge': "Those who know their Dao are in accordance with Heaven. Those who do not know their Dao are in accordance with man."

127 The two central terms in this passage 'partiality,' Chin. *si*私, and 'impartiality,' Chin. *gong*公, could also be translated as 'selfishness' and 'fairness.' However, both the *Yinfu jing* and the commentary on it indicate that Heaven would never act selfishly. The partiality of Heaven that the commentary discusses has nothing to do with unfairness. Indeed, even when Heaven shows partiality, it is only reacting to man's improper actions.

The control of birds lies in *qi*. (DZ 122.14b-15a)

The control of birds:
Unusually victorious among the one hundred birds is the red phoenix[128] from the southern Mountains. When it enters[129] the light and pure *qi*, the inner nature becomes numinous, and thus it will ride with the winds and enter the nine clouds.

As far as the *qi* is concerned, if it is corrupted, it will sink down to earth. If it is pure, it will rise up to Heaven. Therefore, below there is corruption, and above there is purity.

The turtle inhales *qian*.[130] The northern sea spits out the light and pure primordial *qi* eight hundred and ten zhang far. And thus it adds up to the number of nine times nine Yang. The three inches[131] of the birds are in harmony, mutually connected with the primordial *qi*, and are not dispersed.

The *qi* communicates with the spirits. The spirits communicate with the Dao, and the Dao communicates with spontaneity.

Life is the root of death; death is the root of life. Mercy arises in harm; harm arises in mercy. (DZ 122.15a-b)

Life is the root of death:
When the worldly men pursue greed in life, there are plenty of profits, and thus they harm [their] bodies and enter the road of death.

Death is the root of life:
When one embraces the Dao and does not pursue [profits in] life, there is plenty of virtue, and thus he completes his body and enters the road of life. As for the deluded, during the daytime they amass worldly treasures and during the nighttime they destroy the inner gem. As for those who have realized [the Dao], when they sit, they forget the worldly dream; when they lie down, they guard inner perfection.

---

128 The red phoenix, also sometimes translated as the ''vermillion sparrow', is the emblematic creature of the South. Among the organs, it is the heart (the mind) that corresponds to the South.
129 Lit. 'penetrates,' Chin. *tong*通.
130 Chin. 乾, Heaven, the first of the eight trigrams.
131 Chin. *sancun*三寸. It is not entirely clear what Liu Chuxuan is referring to here. The term is sometimes used to designate the three cinnabar fields in the abdomen, the chest and the forehead.

Mercy arises in harm:
The mercy and compassion of the seven sentiments reside in falsity [false action]. And the six thieves secretly harm perfection.

Harm arises in mercy:
"Harm arises" means that the sword of intelligence [can] sever the [sentiments of] love and desire; "in mercy" means that those who have attained the Dao know the mercy of Heaven. Feeding like a fledgling, man has no harm; dwelling like the quail, there will be no mercy in the sentiments.[132]

Ignorant men consider the patterns of Heaven and Earth to be [the substance of] sagacity. I consider the patterns of time and matter to be [the substance] of knowledge. (DZ 122.15b-16b)

Ignorant men consider the patterns of Heaven and Earth to be [the substance of] sagacity:
As for the ignorant man, he destroys [his] existence. He supplicates himself to Heaven [in order to] pursue peace. He always accumulates faults and prays to the saints [in order to] pursue a good fortune. As to the wise man, he knows how to preserve [his] existence, and thus his spirits are mighty. He has no sins, and hence the fortune of Dao will be plentiful.

When a man is corrupt and evil, Heaven and Earth will let the appropriate calamities befall him. When a man is pure and good, sages and saints grant him the appropriate blessings. All living beings on Great Earth create their own karma. They do not change, but they pray to saints and sages. The ten thousand calamities can hardly be avoided. When all men and women of China venerate perfection and are determined not to offer sacrifices to Heaven and Earth, virtue and luck will always arrive.

I consider the patterns and principles of time and matter to be [the substance] of knowledge:
As for the word "I", in the twelve hours of the orbiting Heaven I exhaust the transformations of the ten thousand creatures. As for the word "patterns", [the patterns] reveal the ten thousand ornaments in a splendid way. As for the word "principles," [the principles] reveal the ten thousand communications in an enlightening way. As for the word "wisdom," the ultimate explications are the ten thousand trans-

---

132 This sentence recalls a famous sentence from the *Zhuangzi*. In the Heaven and Earth-chapter (Chin. *tiandi* 天地) we find: "The sage finds his dwelling like a quail (without any choice of his own) and is fed like the fledgling; he is like the bird that passes on (through the air) and leaves no trace of his flight." See James Legge (transl.), *The Texts of Taoism*, New York: The Julian Press Inc., 1959, p.362.

formations, spontaneity, purity and tranquility and the non-acting [wuwei]. Thusness, this is the Dao. Purity, this is Heaven. Quiescence, this is Earth. Non-being, this is when inner nature and existence are the same body. Action, this is when mercy is exercised and no compensation expected.[133] The creation of the ten thousand creatures and the creation of man are not different.[134] Heaven and Earth let the *qi* circulate, and the material substance becomes thoroughly transformed. When the jade tripod lets lead steam, then the gold-furnace refines mercury. The seven reversions let one communicate with the numinous. The nine regenerations permit the elixirs to congeal.[135] The young girl[136] is the *li*-palace, and thus the infant-child[137] is the *kun*-window.[138] Turtle and snake spiral up, and thus tiger and dragon roar.[139] The vermillion quail walks forward, and thus the dark warrior follows suit. The golden father[140]

---

133 Here, Liu Chuxuan gives a two-step analysis of one of the key concepts in both philosophical and religious Daoism, the concept of non-acting, Chin. *wuwei* 無爲. First, he analyses the word *wu*, translated here as "non-being." Second, he explains *wei*, translated here as "action." The concept originated from the *Daodejing* and has ever since been a central focus in Daoist thought. See the fourth chapter of this study.

134 Liu Chuxuan is probably referring to the equation of macrocosmic and microcosmic processes.

135 The 'seven reversions,' Chin. *qifan* 七返, and the 'nine regenerations,' Chin. *jiuhuan* 九還, are key concepts in *inner alchemy*. They occur frequently and generally signify techniques and practices of the circulation of *qi*. The term itself is derived from the *Zhouyi cantong qi*. See ZHDJDC, p.1239.

136 Chin. *chanü* 妊女. DZ 1158, 1b, furnishes the following definiton: "The young girl, that is the lungs."

137 Chin. *ying'er* 嬰兒. In DZ 244, 1.4a, a chart has the following explanation: "The *qi* of the kidneys is called 'infant-child.'" DZ 1158, 1b, has: "The infant-child, that is the lungs."

138 For the significance of the two trigrams *li* and *kun* in *inner alchemy* see the first chapter of this study.

139 In *inner alchemy*, the dragon can symbolize mercury, the spirit and inner nature; the tiger symbolizes lead or *qi*. In DZ 244 *Dadan zhizhi*, 1.6a, we find the following explanations: "The secret method says: The dragon is the correct *qi* above the fluids of the mind. Control it so that it would not rise and disappear. If it meets the *qi* of the kidneys, they would blend spontaneously. The tiger is the water of the perfect one in the *qi* of the kidneys. Control it so that it would not sink down and leave. If it met with the fluids of the mind, they would unite spontaneously." In DZ 1158 *Chongyang shou danyang ershisi jue*, 1b, the dragon is defined as inner nature, the tiger as physical existence.

140 The "golden father," Chin. *jinweng* 金翁, refers to the *qi* arising in the lungs. See ZHDJDCD, p.1217. Also see the chart in DZ 244, 3a: "The *qi* of the lungs is called golden father." In DZ 1158 *Chongyang zhenren shou danyang erhisi jue*, 1b, Chongyang defines the related term *jingong* 金公 as the heart.

guards *geng-xin*,[141] and thus the yellow woman[142] associates with *jia-ji*. Recover from the vast seas, and then chisel jade from the *kun*-mountains.[143] The yellow buds grow, and thus the white snow arises.[144] The jade-flowers are blooming, and thus the gold-lotus[145] blossoms. The three beams illuminate, and thus the seven treasures are shining.[146] The two-eight[147] is without deficiency, and thus the three-six is without losses. The elements metal and wood stand side-by-side, and thus the elements water and fire meet each other. In the total confusion, [the difference] of seclusion and revelation can hardly be estimated.

And this is the application of the Dao.

---

141 *Geng-xin* is the secret name of the yellow metal. In the theory of the five elements, the two celestial stems *geng* and *xin* belong to the elements metal. See DZ 1185 *Baopuzi neipian*抱朴子內篇, 16.1a and ZHDJDCD, p. 1362 and 1378.

142 DZ 1158, 1b: "The yellow woman (Chin. *huangpo*黃婆), this is the abdomen."

143 It is unclear what Liu Chuxuan is referring to here. I could not identify those two terms in any other related texts. However, the choice of metaphors here depicts the supernatural capabilities of the sages. They can travel the seas and the highest mountains and hence the entire world.

144 Both the terms yellow buds, Chin. *huangya*黃芽, and white snow, Chin. *baixue* 白雪, refer to the one *qi* of the former Heaven, Chin. *xiantian*先天. See *ZHDJDCD*, p.1205 and p. 1210. For a description of the cosmogonic processes associated with the one *qi* of Heaven, see the quote taken from DZ 244 *Dadan zhizhi* in the first chapter of this study.

145 The gold-lotus is an important symbol in *Quanzhen* Daoism. It refers to the attainment of immortality or the Dao. *Outer alchemy* used a plant named the gold-lotus for the amalgamation of elixirs. See ZHDJDCD, p.1415.

146 There are different listings of the "seven treasures," Chin. *qibao*七寶. Sometimes the listing comprises the essences, the blood, the *qi*, the marrow, the kidneys and the heart; sometimes the spirits, the veins, the essences, the blood, the saliva and the water. In any case, they represent the entire body. See *ZHDJDCD*, p. 1135.

147 For the meaning of the term "two-eight" see fn. 102.

DZ 122 Huangdi yinfujing zhu

DZ 122 Huangdi yinfujing zhu

DZ 122, 1

黃帝陰符經註

長生子劉處玄註

神仙抱一演道章上

觀天之道執天之行盡矣

觀者五眼圓明也明其天眼慧眼法眼道眼神眼五光明徹則五蘊歸空見其天道也天中復有天外天在地之上清炁天也至高八萬四千里高天也在人身各受天之一炁炁有厚薄沖和則生賢聖逆而散則沉下鬼道者天地萬物之外虛无之體一切眾生悟天之道理盡而明矣要人萬事不憎不愛如天之平等人之有情悟天之無情便是報天之恩也若不依天理縱濁惡邪婬多病夭壽死沉地獄受苦盡則墮於傍生失其人身若依天之道常善則炁和常清則明性常忘情則保命常無涂

DZ 122, 2

則明道常不犯天條則無罪不修世福抱
道全其真福不媅傍門小法頌明无為萬
法所以三界無拘盡矣

天有五賊見之者昌

天有五賊者天無賊非世之盜賊亦非人
之六賊却是甚賊也天有五方正炁在人
身中為神之母也周天十二時中自然抽
添運轉至妙無窮謂之無中有天地傳陰
陽秀炁生於萬物人食五穀養形浮穢沉
於水火五穀之精在人身中保而為命也
命得性而久性得命而壽命者北海之烏
龜也丁翁常抱則成形真陽也

天之真陽見其真陰五賊盜其北海之寶
寶之者昌如萬物人之盜也

五賊在心施行於天宇宙在乎手萬化生乎
身

五賊在心者五行顛倒也在心則眞水上
昇也逆則心毅不通腎水下行死路也世
之不達聖人之道不行道之人皆如此古
之悟道賢達之士多異說世人各執所見

DZ 122, 3

分別高低正能容邪多謗正邪法余觀
恰似螢蟲之耀正道有似日月之光輝
則微光且顯若見日月之光輝照徧十方
三界當見螢耀也聖人掌握宇宙陰陽變
通地天交泰萬化生乎身萬化成形也萬
物之中唯人一物至尊至貴也奪造化內
修身外之身謂之得道通萬化外教物哀
衆生悟金枷玉杻石火風燈世之夢幻途
濁惡而近於清善外應人道內行太上祖
佛之真趣萬法歸一混世而性如蓮出水
謂之全其德此乃上仙萬化之明達也

天性人也人心機也立天之道以定人也

人之天性各有善惡巨微所慕文武道俗
貴賤高下人之性自古至今投胎換殼販
骨更形如蟻巡環未嘗暫止人心之機日
常萬變各有巧拙正邪深淺慈毒孝逆寬
窄長短清濁賢愚愛憎是非察其心機則
知人性也立天之道天之道以定人之
恩大春溫夏煖秋涼冬寒四時而變態生
成萬物濟於人世富貴有錦衣美饌貧賤

DZ 122, 4

富國安民演法章中

天生天殺道之理也天地萬物之盜萬物人之盜人萬物之盜三盜既宜三才既安天生天殺者春溫和煞天生於萬物至秋深金風動萬物枯槁天殺也生殺道理天无情而自然也天地萬物之盜天地四時而變通造化生成萬物萬物之中所藏天地陰陽之秀炁萬物所盜秀炁也萬物人之盜人所盜無窮至寶造化成形世之盜既宜所盜無窮至寶造化成形世之盜人若棄世而悟無情則外物不能所盜欲萬物之華景眼觀五色耳聽五音舌餐五味醉飽腥羶縱邪生婬喪命樂極則衰人若棄世而悟無情則外物不能所盜珉欲念清靜保守命也人萬物之盜人所藏保守命也人萬物之盜人所
三聖教明三乘玄悟三皇上運三光倒推三車耕透三田周天三火爐結三丹神現三陽昇上三天真而不朽生而不滅盡於物道也真與道同體則安也
故曰食其時百骸理動其機萬化安人知其

DZ 122, 5

天人合發萬變定基

頓明至道悟徹萬物之有謂之陽殺其陰性如皓月如心清似天萬里無雲自然光顯森羅萬象人發殺機散盡群陰自然清炁靜陰陽顛倒天地反覆造化生成三丹而結出天地之殼蛻形顯身外真身天人者人性通於天也合發則心盡明知榮枯寵辱成敗也人道通徹人間世夢明知榮枯寵辱成敗禍福衰樂生死古今之常事也人通天理真榮而不枯真寵而不辱真成而不敗真福而不禍真樂而不哀真生而不死明道之常也道常通而通萬變定其性之基本也至性通極無物萬變自然萬通如上善方圓曲直萬派清通於江河淮濟入巨洋而混成歸一謂之深通

性有巧拙可以伏藏

古之悟道之人內性善巧方便衰人外如惡拙可以伏藏內光隱而不顯也河上公云如美玉處石似明珠在蚌蛤禽之異巧驚能語鐵籠拘四拙鳩訥聲萬枝縱橫所

DZ 122, 6

以世人偽巧則生萬禍真拙則生於清福
故天不言而自然變通天道忘言而自然忘
老人要明於天道忘言則窮造化之妙忘
情則明旦古之容人之所欲多巧則多慾
多情則多患忘世斷情則乃樂道保命之
要

九竅之邪在乎三要可以動靜
九竅九通之陽徑未通者九陰之邪鳥也
人心方寸空虛內有靈內上人心有九竅
中人七竅下人五竅心無竅謂之愚人邪
陰生性濁陽耀降神清在乎三要天光有
日月星地實有金玉珍寶通有鉛汞真可
以動靜天動則三光照地靜則三寶通妙
明則三靈結動者動於形也靜者靜於性
也古之賢隱混世而不動心居山而不著
靜形明有有動中有靜中宣動靜
俱忘則得道之常妙也
火生於木禍發必剋姦生於國時動必潰
之修鍊謂之聖人
火生人之心日常觸處榮萬變之惡於木

DZ 122, 7

者乃人性也念發無明火則焚其木之性
也禍發必剋違吉而凶喪福也剋者
被於真也姦生於國以智治國國之賊也使詐
治國之福也以智治國太上經云不以智
人生於國難以萬民無事也時動則必潰
散也愚者非理亂於世必遭刑法也不以
智治國以無事治天下太平民安也知之
修鍊非燒五金八石之修鍊修性命則達
理通玄三教謂之悟道常救物哀世知天
愚而謂之積德自黃帝之悟道有此陰符
經周時金輪王悟釋有此金剛經自成佛
之後號釋迦年尼佛金剛經三十二分言
其道要除我相人相眾生相壽者相無四
相心上無無慾也如天無雲性如朗月自
現圓明正性也性者如樹之根也身者如
人之形也萬法者如樹枝葉也陰符經造
化之趣通其理各分別執根梢枝葉開花結子
各執自是他非有四相心未除謂之傍門
也

DZ 122, 8

富國安民演法章中

天生天殺道之理也天地萬物之盜萬物人
之盜人萬物之盜三盜既宜三才既安
天生天殺者春溫和而煞天生於萬物至秋
深金風動萬物枯槁天殺也生殺道理天
之盜人所盜萬物之秀炁也萬物人
之盜人所盜萬物之精拿天地之秀炁而
泯欲念清靜保守命也人萬物之盜人所
而變通造化生成萬物之中所藏天
地陰陽之秀炁禀於也萬物人
无情而自然也天地萬物之盜天地四時
欲萬物之華景眼觀五色耳聽五音舌餐
五味醉飽腥羶殺邪生婬喪命樂極則哀
人若棄世而悟無情則外物不能所盜
三盜既宜所盜無窮至寶造化成形世之
萬解珠珍難以酬價賞也三才既安歸依
三聖教明三乘玄悟三皇上運三光倒推
三車耕透三田周天三火爐結三丹神現
三陽昇上三天真而不朽生而不滅盡於
物道也真與道同體則安也
故曰食其時百骸理動其機萬化安人知其

DZ 122, 9

神而神不知不神而所以神也
食其時饑時遇美饌而不愛逢擾食而不
嫌也不殺生食羶腥亦不修齋餐瑩素但
饑時不論麤細困時唱快時吟要
坐則坐要臥則臥要住則住要行則行敎
四大無拘自在則百骸理也十二時中對
萬景只要真心湛然動者不可動於心
也內現寶光應物動於形機者聖人賢人
君子謂之智將軍謂之計常人謂之機小
人謂之脫空聖人為智大理深世人不能
盡明其理懷妙智口應常機信者聽善者
從萬通闢化頓悟則安靜道生也人知其
神而神世人只知地祇陰神而神也以未
雕泥捏神為神愚者不知凡造一分慇過
則天降一分禍患殺害豬羊廣燒錢馬祈
禱有病則求安有禍則求福不知不神而
所以神也不知天上陽道至神各分方位
暗察人間善惡世人造善三年不經三年
而降吉祥世人若造惡千日不經三年而降
禍患世人不知萬物之中最靈最通者自

DZ 122, 10

己元神有通天徹地輝耀古之賢聖盡是
悟道修真從凡入聖西天一佛至二十八
代佛未修行時都是衆生為人之性也性
眼圓明泯四相名為佛佛者人之性也性
者神性是神神性只是異名釋門性性除

四相謂之佛道門神忘四相謂之仙
日月有數大小有定聖功生焉神明出焉
人之命也男子十六歲至二八真金若
不悟無情三年減一兩至八八六十四卦
盡則腎海枯竭也多欲未盡而夭壽
日生酉時西山日墜清靜經云大道無情
運行日月者慧光運而抽添有數月
節減欲則盈壽延長盈而虧則人夭而
不缺則人生大小有大包
含天地小者微也論微之妙入於毫芒
而天地不能量用而鬼神不能見自然有
定於方寸聖功生焉天之道也天大恩生
濟人養形道聖功生故人修真神明出焉

DZ 122, 11

隱而神遊於三宮顯而神通於八表
其盜機也天下莫能見莫能知君子得之固
窮小人得之輕命
其盜機也萬物之機所盜天地之炁天下
莫能見天大恩生莫能知愚者只知自能
養其身不知天垂恩而養萬民春種秋收
夏結冬藏應時霜雪雨露滋榮萬化世之
知天恩者性通明達也君子得之固窮窮
通道則天地通則萬化通萬化通
則神通神通則應機萬變抱一無離而閒
然顧真返朴小人得之輕命小人得時欺
謾天地不敬賢聖不遵國法不仁不義自
強他弱害物傷人怨極則天報君子重性
得通賢聖小人輕命失墜傍生
強兵戰勝演術章下
瞽者善聽賢者善視絕利一源用師十倍三
反晝夜用師萬倍
瞽者善聽賢人之目乃五臟之看竅也通風
則覩於外物也如紙席僻風相隔似瞽者
不能見外物也外景不入於中則空中有

DZ 122, 12

真聲真仙善聽無聲之聲也耳者善視世
之俗氣到耳則如聲也道念到耳竅通也
言者亦如聲也正理擇其善者耳窺通也
似鑿壁透外光入於中也視無物之物乃
明恍惚之妙也絕利一源忘貪而清平也
亦泯利貯財損有餘而惠不足也用師十
倍至聞明有十倍功利物受人有十倍福
三反晝夜一反上元賜福氣降而靈也二
反中元赦罪神異而靈也三下元解厄
命通陰變為陽也用師萬倍世人興販物
貨萬苦千辛更廣有利者難取一倍利悟
道修真全其性命得無窮福壽佳仙宮寶
所受天上富貴譬愉人之求福利則及萬
倍便海變桑田永居不夜之鄉真樂何至
只萬倍利也

心生於物死於物機在目
心生於物著於物外也死於心死則通於
靈物也世求生則性歸死路達道則守死
神遊生路道與俗生死路異相違也
在目外目視於物心動於機也利而有害

DZ 122, 13

貪而有爭也慧目視物明於天機知道
要妙物我俱泯也俗機益於已損於人道
機損於已益於人也
天之無恩而大恩生物迅雷烈風莫不蠢然
天之無恩布氣生物而不有而大恩生萬
物生成也萬物不得天地之炁不能造化
成形天大恩生物若無恩者天不望其報也
人恩見其有者望其報也天恩與人恩
異也迅雷鳴則甘雨降天地生萌烈風動
則浮雲散萬里天青莫不蠢然動舍靈
胎卵濕化莫不總受天之一炁生何況萬
物之無情之物
至樂性餘至靜性廉
常樂道性之有餘我無喜
則無憂人有歡則有愁悟恬淡得之真常
迷靜色失之幻夢至靜性廉至靜則盡於
物也性廉不著於水也達道之人居
塵不染在欲無欲磨開寶鏡應物之形影
何礙有一等不達中邊悟道之螢燿認至
靜棄有著無有取捨之妄想分別高下誇

DZ 122, 14

天之至私用之至公也

天施恩不令下知至私也生成濟於人世至公也人之有道如石中藏玉世之肉眼未見其珍頻磨頻琢異日功成現身外之身朴散成於大器人之無道似蠹木之樹天眼有日見用斧用鋸片時朽爛詭得魂飛蠅散濁性永墮幽冥修道衰世苦盡甘來造惡福謝萬禍臨身天意順者逆行逆者順行君子上賢達榮於道德天報預至私盡至公小人之下匹夫競於色財天報先至公終至私

禽之制在炁

禽之制百禽異勝者南山赤鳳也通輕清之炁性靈風入於九霄在炁濁則沉地清則昇天因下濁而上清烏龜吸乾坤海吐輕清元炁八百一十丈乃九九之陽

DZ 122, 15

恩

生者死之根死者生之根恩生於害害生於恩

數也禽之三寸沖和與元炁相接不散炁通神·神通道道自然

入於死路也死者生之根抱道不求生德多則全身入於生路也迷者晝食世實夜喪內珍悟者坐忘世夢卧守內真恩生於害七情恩憐於偽六賊晴害於真害生於恩害生者慧劍斷愛欲也於恩者達道知

天恩也穀食則人無害鵲居則情無恩愚人以天地文理聖我以時物文理哲愚人以天地文理聖我以時物文理哲日常積德禱聖求福賢者喪命保吉天永安靈無罪則道福洪人濁惡天降其禍人清善聖賢賜其禧大地眾生總造業不改禱聖賢為禍難免中華女男都崇真有志不祈天善福常侵我以時物文理哲我以周天十二時窮萬物之變文俊顯萬華理明顯萬通哲極聞萬化自然清靜無為

黃帝陰符經註 終

也自然道也清者天也靜者地也无者性與道體同也為者施恩不望其報也天地運無物造化與人造化無異也天地運無物通變也玉鼎烹鉛則金爐鍊汞也七返通靈九還丹結姹女離宮則嬰兒坎戶也竈蛇蟠遶則龍虎咆哮也前朱雀行則後玄武隨也金翁守庚辛則黃婆伴甲乙也巨海撈金則崑山磐玉也黃芽長則白雪生也玉花開則金蓮結也三光照則七寶明也二八無虧則六三無缺也金木間隔則水火相逢也恍惚之中則隱顯難測也道之用也

Bibliography

Abbreviations

DZ	*Daozang* (The Daoist Canon)
DJDCD	*Daojiao dacidian*
HJOAS	*Harvard Journal of Asiatic Studies*
MS	*Monumenta Serica*
NOAG	*Nachrichten der Gesellschaft für Natur- und Völkerkunde Ostasiens, Hamburg*
OE	*Orient Extremus*
SJZJYJ	*Shijie zongjiao yanjiu*
T.	Taisho shinshu daizokyo (The Buddhist Canon), Tokyo 1924-1929
TP	*T'oung Pao*
ZDCD	*Zhonghua daojiao dacidian*
ZDMG	*Zeitschrift der Deutschen Morgenländischen Gesellschaft*

1. Primary Sources from the Daoist Canon

DZ 31	*Huangdi yinfu jing*
DZ 110	*Huangdi yinfu jing shu*
DZ 121	*Huangdi yinfu jing zhu*
DZ 122	*Huangdi yinfu jing zhu*
DZ 173	*Jinlian zhengzong ji*
DZ 174	*Jinlian zhengzong xianyuan xiangzhuan*
DZ 175	*Qizhen nianpu*
DZ 244	*Dadan zhizhi*
DZ 297	*Lishi zhenxian tidao tongjian xupian*
DZ 393	*Daode zhenjing zhu*
DZ 401	*Huangting neijing yujing zhu*
DZ 620	*Qingjing miaojing*
DZ 664	*Daode zhenjing*
DZ 682	*Daode zhenjing zhu*

DZ 768   *Tujingyanyi bencao*
DZ 973   *Ganshui xianyuan lu*
DZ 1008 *Zhouyi cantong qi*
DZ 1032 *Yunji qiqian*
DZ 1056 *Jin zhenren yulu*
DZ 1057 *Danyang zhenren yulu*
DZ 1058 *Wuwei qingjing changsheng zhenren yulu*
DZ 1123 *Miaomen youxi*
DZ 1141 *Xianle ji*
DZ 1153 *Chongyang quanzhen ji*
DZ 1154 *Chongyang jiaohua ji*
DZ 1156 *Chongyang zhenren jinguan yusuo*
DZ 1157 *Chongyang shou danyang ershisi jue*
DZ 1161 *Taigu ji*
DZ 1185 *Baopuzi neipian*
DZ 1233 *Chongyang lijiao shiwu lun*
DZ 1205 *Santian neijie jing*
DZ 1256 *Zhenxian zhizhi yulu*
DZ 1437 *Taishang laojun kaitian jing*

2. Other Chinese Sources

Chen Yuan, et al., eds. *Daojia jinshi lüe*. Beijing: Wenwu, 1988.
Ch'I Ssu-ho, ed. Chuang-tzu-yin-te. Beiping: Ha-fo-yen-ching, 1948.
Siku quanshu zongmu, 2 vols. Beijing: Zhonghua shuju, 1965.
Jingang panruo poluomijing. T. 235.

3. Secondary Literature in Chinese

Chen Bing. *Lüelun quanzhendao de sanjiao heyi shuo*. In: *Shijie zongjiao yanjiu*, 1.1984.
Chen Houmin. *Lüelun quanzhendao de sixiang yuanliu*. In: *Shijie zongjiao yanjiu*, 3.1983.
Ciyuan. Beijing: Shangwu yinshuguan, 1998.
Daojiao dacidian. Beijing: Xinhua shudian 1994.
Gong Pengcheng. *Daojiao xinlun*. Taibei: Taiwan xuesheng 1990.
Huang Taohan. *Quanzhen qizi ci shuping*. In: Xianggang zhongwen daxue zhongguo wenhua yanjiusuo xuebao, 19, 1988.

Li Yuanguo. *Daojiao qigong yangsheng xue*. Chengdu: Sichuansheng shehue kexueyuan chubanshe, 1988.
Weng Dujian. *Daozang zimu yinde*. Beiping: Ho-fo-yen-ching, 1935.
Zhang Guangbao. *Jinyuan quanzhendao neidan xinxinglun yanjiu*. Taibei: Wenjian, 1993.
Zhonghua daojiao dacidian. Beijing: Zhongguo shehui kexue chubanshe, 1995.
Zhongwen dacidian (8 vol.). Taibei, 1972-1980.

4. Secondary literature in Western languages

Baldrian-Hussein, Farzeen. *Inner Alchemy: Notes on the Origin and Use of the Term Neidan*. In: Cahiers d'extreme-asie, 1989. Vol. 5.
Belamido, Paulino T. *Self-Cultivation and Quanzhen Daoism with Special Reference to the Legacy of Qiu Chuji*. Michigan: UMI, 2002.
Berling, Judith A. *Paths of Convergence: Interactions of Inner Alchemy Taoism and Neo-Confucianism*. In: Journal of Chinese Philosophy 1979. Vol. 6.
Boehmer, Thomas. *Taoist Alchemy: A Sympathetic Approach through Symbols*. In: Saso, Michael R. and David W. Chappel, eds. Buddhist and Taoist Studies I. Hawaii: Asian Studies at Hawaii; no. 18, University Press of Hawaii, 1997.
Boltz, Judith. *A Survey of Taoist Literature, Tenth to Seventeenth Century*. Berkeley: University of Berkeley Press, 1987.
Chan, Wing-tsit. *A Source Book in Chinese Philosophy*. Princeton: Princeton University Press, 1973.
Chan, Alan K.L. *A Tale of Two Commentaries: Ho-Shang-Kong and Wang-Pi on the Lao-Tzu*. In: Livia Kohn and Michael LaFargue, eds. *Lao-tzu and the Tao-te-ching*. New York, 1998.
Ching, Julia. *The Religious Thought of Chu Hsi*. New York 2000: Oxford University Press, 2000.
Cleary, Thomas. *Vitality, Energy, Spirit, A Taoist Sourcebook*: Boston and London, 1991.
Demiéville, Paul. *La Situation Religieuse en Chine au Temps de Marco Polo*. In: Oriente Poliano, 1957.
Eskildsen, Stephen E. *The Beliefs and Practices of Early Chüan-Chen Taoism*. Master's thesis at the University of British Columbia, 1986. Ottawa: Canadian Thesis Service.
— *The Teachings and Practices of the Early Quanzhen Taoist Masters*. New York: State University of New York Press, 2004.

Franke, Herbert. *The Chin dynasty*. In: Herbert Franke and Denis Twitchett, eds. *The Cambridge History of China. Vol.6: Alien Regimes and Border States, 907-1368*, Cambridge: Cambridge University Press, 1984.

Max Kaltenmark, "The Ideology of the *T'ai-p'ing ching.*" In: Holmes Welch and Anna Siedel, eds. *Facets of Taoism*. New Haven, 1979

Kohn, Livia. *The Taoist Experience*. New York, 1993.

— *God of the Dao*. Ann Arbor: University of Michigan Press, 1998.

— (ed.). *Daoist Handbook*. Leiden, Boston, Köln: Brill, 2000.

— (ed.). *Taoist Meditation and Longevity Techniques*. Ann Arbor: Center for Chinese Studies, The University of Michigan, 1989.

Legge, James. *The Texts of Taoism*. New York: The Julian Press, 1959.

Masaaki, Tsuchiya. *Confessions of Sins and Awarness of Self in the Taiping jing*. In: Livia Kohn and Harold D. Roth, eds. *Daoist Identity: History, Lineage and Ritual*. Hawaii: Hawaii University Press, 2002

Needham, Joseph and Lu Gwei-Djen. *Science and Civilisation in China: Vol.5 V*. Taipei: Caves Books, Ltd., 1986.

Porkert, Manfred. *Die theoretischen Grundlagen der chinesischen Medizin*. Stuttgart: S. Hirzel Verlag, 1982.

Pulleyblank, Edwin G. *Outline of Classical Chinese Grammar*. Vancouver: UBC press, 1995.

Pas, Julian F. and Man Kam Leung. *Historical Dictionary of Taoism*. Lanham, Md. and London: The Scarecrow Press, 1998.

Rand, Christopher C. *Li Ch'uan and Chinese Military Thought*. In: HJOAS, Vol. 39, Issue 1, June 1979.

Reiter, Florian C. *The Soothsayer Hao Ta/t'ung (1140-1212) and his Encounter with Ch'üan-chen Taoism*. In: Oriens Extremus, Heft 2, 1981.

— *The "Scripture of the Hidden Contracts" (Yin-fu ching), a Short Survey on Facts and Findings*. In: NOAG/Hamburg, 136, 1984.

— *Chung-Yang Sets Forth his Teachings in Fourteen Discourses*. In: MS 36, 1984-85.

— *Grundelemente des religiösen Taoismus: Das Spannungsverhältnis von Integration und Individualität in seiner Geschichte zur Chin-, Yüan- und frühen Ming-Zeit*. Stuttgart: Franz Steiner Verlag Wiesbaden GmbH, 1988.

— *Überlegungen zur Bedeutung des Buddhismus für den Chüan-chen-Taoismus im China des 12. und 13. Jahrhunderts*. In: MS 42, 1994.

— *The Ch'üan-chen Patriarch T'an Ch'u-tuan (1123 – 1185) and the Chinese Talismanic Tradition*. In: ZDMG 146.

— *The Blending of Religious Convictions and Scholarly Notions in the Life of the Taoist Patriarch Liu Ch'u-hsüan (1147 – 1203)*. In: YDMG, Band 147, Heft 2, 1997.
Robinet, Isabel. *Taoist Meditation: The Mao-Shan Tradition of Great Purity*. Albany: State University of New York Press 1993.
— *Taoism: Growth of a Religion*. Stanford 1997: Stanford University Press.
Saso, Michael R. *Taoism and the Rite of Cosmic Renewal.* Washington: WSU Press, 1990.
— *The Gold Pavilion: Taoist Ways to Peace, Healing and Long Life*. Boston, Rutland, Vermont, Tokyo: Charles E. Tuttle Co., Inc., 1995.
Welch, Holmes and Anna Seidel (ed.). *Facets of Taoism*: *Essays in Chinese Religion*. New Haven and London: Yale University Press, 1979.
Welch, Holmes. *Taoism:The Parting of the Way.*Boston: Bacon Press 1966.
Schipper, Kristofer. Concordance du Tao-tsang. Paris 1975.
— *The Taoist Body (*reprint, *Taipei: SMC Publishing,1993)*
Wu Sing Chow. *A Study of the Taoist Internal Elixir – its Theory and Development*. Ann Arbor: UMI, 1974.
W.A. Soothill, W.A. and L. Hodous. *A Dictionary of Chinese Buddhist Terms* (repr.). Richmond 1995.
Wong, Eva (transl.). *Seven Taoist Masters: A Folk Novel of China*. Boston: Shambhala Publications 1990.
Yao, Tao-chung. *Ch'üan-Chen: A New Taoist Sect In North China During The Twelfth And Thirteenth Centuries*. Dissertation at the University of Arizona: University Microfilm International, 1980.
— *Buddhism and Taoism under the Chin*. In: Tillmann, Hoyt Cleveland and Stephen H. West, *China under Jurchen Rule, Essays on Chin Intellectual History*. Albany: State University of New York Press, 1998.
Yu, David C. (transl.). *History of Chinese Daoism*. London, New York, Oxford: University Press of America, 2000.
Zhang Jiyu and Li Yuanguo. *"Mutual Steeling among the Three Powers" in the Scripture of Unconscious Unification*. In: Girardot, N.J., James Miller and Liu Xiaogan (ed.). *Daoism and Ecology*. Cambridge: Cambridge University Press, 2001.
Zürcher, Erik. *The Buddhist Conquest of China, The Spread and Adaption of Buddhism in Early Medieval China* (2 Vols.). Leiden 1959: E.Brill.
— Buddhist Influences on Early Taoism, in: TP, Vol. LXVI (1980).